The Crown Jewel of Shankara

newly mounted
by Bernd Helge Fritsch

Translation from Sanskrit: Swami Pulpul Govinanda

English translation from German: Peter Hessel,
Delmenhorst, Germany, www.peterhesseltranslator.com

Cover: Bernd Helge Fritsch
Layout: Dr. Evelyn Schmelzer

Illustrations in the book:
Harry Schiffer
Evelyn Schmelzer
Karin Wimmer

Produced and published by
BoD - Books on Demand,
Norderstedt
ISBN 9783738626285

The author

Originally, Bernd Helge Fritsch was a successful lawyer. Following an inner voice, he gave up his law practice shortly after turning forty.

He spent many years travelling in Asia and southern Europe, lived in Buddhist and Hindu monasteries, studied and practiced Zen.

For the last thirty years or so he has been lecturing throughout Europe.

Particularly his books, "Der große Prinz und das Glück", "Wu Wei", "Das Kleinod des Shankara"and "The Essence of the Bhagavad Gita" have made Bernd H. Fritsch well-known to a large readership as an inspiring author.

The book

Adi Shankara (788-820 A.D.) is regarded as the most impor-
tant Indian spiritual philosopher and reformer of Hinduism.
His famous major work was "Viveka Chudamani" (Jewel of
Distinction)[1]. It is considered the "crown jewel" of Ancient
Indian wisdom.

The present edition offers the reader a modern translation
of the "Jewel" and a careful selection from the originally 580
Sanskrit verses. The author has left out numerous repetitive
passages as well as statements not in keeping with our modern *zeitgeist*.

Explanations have been added to many verses by Bernd Helge
Fritsch, a spiritual teacher himself. They serve to clarify the
meaning of Shankara's text which is now approximately 1200
years old.

This book deals with the central questions of our life: "What
constitutes the meaning of my life? How do we explain our destiny? How do we liberate ourselves from worries, illness and
suffering? How can we connect ourselves with the everlasting
beauty, love and bliss at the fundamental basis of Being?

---

[1] In earlier English-language literature, Vivela Chudamani was trans-
lated as "Crest Jewel of Discrimination" or "Crown Jewel of Discrimination". The translator considers "Crown Jewel of Distinction" more appro-
priate, since the word "discrimination" has undergone a transformation
and now means primarily the prejudicial treatment of people.

Contents

Introduction

Confessing to belong to a religious denomination, or believing in a religious teaching often has little to do with spirituality. A spiritual person connects with the dimension beyond phenomena that are perceivable with the senses. This person goes beyond the limits of reason that tries to understand the world through intellectual analysis. A spiritual person is not satisfied with others telling him about the primal source of Being. He wants to experience it himself. Yet he appreciates guidelines supported by a transcendental viewpoint. This book, this discussion of Shankara's teachings, should also be regarded as such a guide.

Many pearls of wisdom have been communicated to us by teachers who have immersed themselves deeply in the wonders and secrets of life. We find such pearls in the writings of Hinduism and Buddhism, in the Old and New Testament, in the teachings of Taoism, the Greek philosophers, the words of Christian mystics, Islamic Sufis and many others. All these jewels come from the universal awareness beyond the common intellect. It is reassuring and pleasing that all these sages are basically proclaiming the same message about God and the world, whether they call this "God" Buddha, Allah, Jehovah, Brahman or by any other name.

No one can know the taste of honey without having sampled it. Descriptions alone cannot provide us with the "experience" of honey. Just the same, to reach the level which always was and always will be the source of all sensually perceivable forms, we all must walk the road beyond reason by ourselves.

The "Crown Jewel of Shankara" is not concerned with a "faith" or a certain "creed". It is a highly practical guide teaching us how we can taste the honey and not just speculate about it. To the editor of this book, the "Crown Jewel of Shankara" is one of the most profound descriptions ever given to mankind of the road to the core of our own Being, to the experience of peace, safety and bliss beyond the world of physical manifestations.

Shankara was one of India's great teachers of wisdom. He lived approximately from 788 to 820 A.D. Shankara is said to have written numerous comments on the old Indian scriptures of wisdom (Vedas, Upanishads, Bhagavad-Gita). He represented the Advaita philosophy which teaches that there is only ONE Being, a oneness of all life. All is Brahman (the all-encompassing deity, the universal consciousness). That is why man in his essence is not separated from nature, from other humans and from the all-encompassing Being. Only in man's clouded consciousness does the illusion arise that we are alone and confronted with a world that is often classified as threatening.

The "Crown Jewel of Distinction" (original title: Viveka-Chudamani) is regarded as the best known and most important of Shankara's writings. In it we find the wisdom of Ancient Indian teachings in a nutshell. It consists of 580 Sanskrit verses in which the master explains to his pupil the nature of Atman – every man's immortal soul, and the way to unite with Brahman.

The present edition is reduced to about half the number of original verses. Many repetitions as well as statements not in keeping with the spirit of our time have been left out. Some verses were simplified for the sake of clarity; some others were combined into one verse. Some repetitions were deliberately left in because they well represent the mantra-like, memorable character of the original.

The editor has added supplementary and explanatory comments to many verses.

The journey's destination – Knowledge and immortality

1.   The pupil bows to Govinda and all great teachers of wisdom. These masters remain in a state of supreme bliss. Deeply connected with the all-encompassing Being, they draw their inner images which they then cast into words. They open our hearts to beauty, freedom, peace and love beyond duality.

2.   The master speaks:
To be born as a human is an unparalleled gift.
There are people who have been awarded this precious and rare gift, and yet so lost are they that they make no effort to become liberated. Such people are suicidal. They cling to the unreal, and they destroy themselves.

3.   Knowing holy scriptures elevates us beyond merely being human. The ability to distinguish between the Self (Atman) and the non-Self reflects a high level of evolution. However, liberation can only be attained by consciously becoming one with Brahman. This level of consciousness is not easy to achieve. We require the grace of God, a deep wish for liberation, and instruction by a great master.

Every being is united with Brahman, the all-encompassing deity. We cannot exist except within and through Brahman. Yet man, blinded by a misinterpretation of external forms, may feel to be an isolated individual. That is what causes anxieties and problems.

It is normal for many people that their life is a chain of difficulties and worries. Most will find it quite unrealistic to think that their life is perfect the way it is, in the smallest detail and every moment of the day. In their opinion, the "facts" they can perceive with their senses point far too mightily against it. The human mind derives these alleged "facts" by separating its consciousness from oneness with Atman and Brahman.

4. *People cling to transient phenomena. They fail to achieve their Being. They miss the greatest bliss, the journey's destination, the oneness with universal consciousness, with Brahman.*

We sense that life must be supernaturally beautiful and boundless. Somewhere, at some time, all people in their inner Being have already been able to experience this, at least for some short moments. Yet why is it so difficult to connect continuously with the immeasurable glory and vastness of Being?

All life is permeated by consciousness. This consciousness comes from the dimension beyond external forms. It is the dimension of the unlimited eternal Being.

The invisible all-encompassing consciousness we cannot grasp with our thoughts is the origin of all forms. It is the basic substance of all phenomena. Our thinking, too, is nothing but consciousness. However, this thinking is limited and is the reason why our life feels largely narrow, faulty, full of loss, and transient. This thinking believes in deficiency and does not recognize the perfection of all Being.

It is difficult for the mind to understand that our world is supposed to be perfect and full of divine wisdom. Our mind has no access to the eternal bright dimension behind the phenomena. The transience of external forms, the suffering, illness and death are proof to us that Being is imperfect. But as Zen mistress Joko Beck says: *"Transience is basically just another word for completeness. We must live and die, that is the essence of completeness...*" It is our inner resistance against the Being as it is that clouds our view of its beauty and wisdom.

Nature has completeness to show that it is the reflection of God, and it has flaws to show that it is only a reflection.

Blaise Pascal

5.   *There is no point in studying sacred scriptures, in performing rites and in worshiping deities as long as we don't recognize our true identity. Only those achieve liberation who can behold their oneness with Atman.*

Atman and Brahman are the two key terms, the recurring theme in the "Crown Jewel of Distinction". Brahman means the all-encompassing Being, "the One without a second". Brahman is the great emptiness as well as the entire universe that surrounds us. Emptiness is universal consciousness beyond thought and form. Brahman is the NOTHING and the ALL. It comprises all the unlimited opportunities of Being as well as all concrete phenomena.

Brahman is not this or that. Limiting Brahman to any content contradicts the idea of a comprehensive Being. However, the statement that Brahman is all and nothing exceeds the analytical, logical mind. We can only perceive this reality when reason remains silent.

In its basic essence, Brahman is "pure consciousness", which means consciousness without concrete content. Usually, human consciousness is always connected with an object (such as a sensory perception or a thought). We only experience pure consciousness, the origin of all forms, under exceptional circumstances (such as in meditation).

Brahman from within gives birth to man with his individual core of life (Atman). In its essence, Atman is identical with Brahman.

Corresponding also to the tradition of the Old Testament (Genesis 1:27), man was created in the image of God. Since this man – according to Indian philosophy, confused by the influence of the goddess Maya – identifies with his body, his senses and his mind (thinking, feeling, wanting), an unreal sham – personality results, called the ego. This ego has "forgotten" its original oneness with God. That is the root cause of all its problems.

According to the Hindu teaching of wisdom, the ego soul must suffer and go through constantly changing incarnations until it is completely at one again with Atman and Brahman. That ends its ephemeral, anxious and painful sham – reality that is separated from God and the other human beings. That process is called "liberation" or "enlightenment".

6. No action can give us liberation. Enlightenment and immortality cannot be acquired by hard work, the collection of wealth or by good deeds, but solely through dedication, which means giving up the false identity.

We humans think we have to do something to achieve the fullness of life. The comprehensive Being, which in essence is identical to our personal Being, to our life, is full of splendour and glory. We cannot add anything worthwhile to it. Our primary task in this world is to become more conscious. That means paying close and careful attention to the processes in our mind. Then we recognize the veil of unreality which our limited thinking has draped over reality. As soon as we become aware of this fact, the dense fog lifts, and the Being shines forth in the light of true recognition.

> *7. Those who seek wisdom will stop desiring this or that. They will recognize that they carry the bliss of pure consciousness within them. They will liberate their soul from the floods of external forms, from all the coming and going. That is how they achieve oneness with the origin of life.*

People are only aware of the dualist exterior of phenomena. They have lost their reference to the everlasting and complete dimension of their Being. That is why they only see a small part, a reflection of reality. They observe the constant comings and goings in the external world. That causes worries, anxiety, wishing, hoping and desire.

As a rule, people – due to their superficial point of view – regard their present life situation as inadequate. They constantly feel that something is lacking that keeps them from being happy. This feeling of deficiency drives them to look for change, activity, hard work and effort in the hope that perhaps they may find fulfilment. in the future. That is the cause of stress in our time.

With our desire for this and that, we assume that the all-encompassing universe is incomplete. That is why we chase after happiness we hope to achieve in the future. This approach disables us to plunge into the Being more deeply NOW (there is only the present Being!). Only in the "here and now" can we experience the wisdom, beauty, love and completeness of life.

Thinking deficiency causes deficiency. With the power of our thoughts we attract what we expect. Those who recognize the fullness of Being will be able to enjoy its fruits.

> *8. Righteous action cleanses the heart. But we do not achieve insight into reality with deeds. We recognize true timeless reality by distinguishing between the ephemeral and the everlasting. It is time for your*

> *liberation, too. You are ready to distinguish between the Atman and the non-Atman, between pure consciousness and the world of phenomena.*

Through the right kind of distinction, the pupil becomes one with Atman and Brahman. He does not flee from this world, but he is no longer bound by it. Like Jesus, he can say about himself: *"I live IN this world, but in the knowledge that I am not OF this world"*. With dedication, but always composed, he meets his worldly responsibilities. Whatever the fruits of his labour may be, he is not concerned about them. Without fancying that he must achieve something to be happy, he is at rest within himself.

> 9.   *Only through meditation, supported by wise teachings, will you reach fulfilment. External action such as good deeds, religious practices, or breathing exercises alone cannot make you experience the true Being.*
> *External circumstances such as place and time are of secondary importance. The inner attitude of the seeker decides whether he will reach the goal.*

Contemplation and meditation are the ways of yoga. Yoga means establishing the connection with the spiritual world. In contemplation we become internally serene, allowing spiritual wisdom to penetrate us. We do not try to rationalize this wisdom. We observe it, connect with it and – motivated by it – achieve insight into Being from within.

Contemplation should be distinguished from blind faith. Everyone possesses an inner feeling for truth. The more selflessly we approach the mysteries of life, the better we can intuitively recognize the truth. However, those who deal with spirituality to become "holy" or better than other people, will miss their target and easily lose themselves in dubious "esotericism".

Meditation serves the purpose of observing the stream of thoughts in our own mind and to free ourselves from it. With that, the space beyond our usual concepts becomes accessible.

Whether we reach the goal depends on the seeker's correct inner attitude. Time and place of our effort is of little importance. We don't have to travel anywhere to recognize the truth because it can be found only deep within ourselves.

10. Those who want to know their true nature, should find a teacher who has given up his ego and reposes peacefully in Being.

The whole universe supports your striving to recognize reality. With confidence, you will have the kind of help at the right time that corresponds to the level of your consciousness. You will be helped by people, events, books and other "teachers". The two most important teachers will always be ready for you: on the one hand realization that comes from awareness, and on the other hand suffering caused by your ignorance. You can choose among those two.

As paradox as it may sound, suffering is part of the completion of Being. As many people can confirm based on their own experience: Suffering – properly understood – can serve to challenge us and give us strong motivation to change our attitude in life.

Suffering is the result of karma. The following verses of the "Crown Jewel" will describe in detail how we can go beyond suffering and karma.

The first steps toward liberation

11. The sages have explained the four requirements for achieving liberation.
- *The most important requirement is to distinguish between the eternal and the ephemeral forms;*
- *Next, we must separate ourselves from desiring the fruits of our own labour;*
- *Then, we need inner peace, composure and perseverance;*
- *Last but not least we must have an active longing for liberation.*

The world of forms is ephemeral. Everything flows. What is coming will pass. Even the earth, the sun and all heavenly bodies will disappear. That is why those who adhere to the ephemeral must suffer again and again. Brahman, the pure consciousness, is the truth; the world is an illusion.

Those will achieve recognition who – free of desire – serenely observe what is. This applies to external phenomena as well as to internal life. With this awareness, we liberate ourselves from patterns of thinking and feeling that obscure our view of reality.

The great error consists of believing that any external event, any thing or person will give you lasting peace and permanent blissful Being. The world of forms is not suited for that. Peace and bliss can only be found in the centre of our own Being.

Another requirement for achieving deep peace is composure toward the fruits of your labour. Fruits may grow or not. What comes will come; what does not, will not. Learn to take life as it is and to make the best of it. That is how harmony fulfills the Being.

The karma of doing –
Bad deeds have bad consequences;
Good deeds have good consequences;
Doing for the sake of doing
Has no consequences at all.

Siddharta Gautama Buddha

12. Distinction (Viveka) is to differentiate between
what is eternal and what is ephemeral. The object is to
recognize that Brahman is the only true reality, and that
the external world is only an illusionary reality.

13. You will reach the liberated state of dispassion
when you recognize that all forms – from the body to
possessions and to mental concepts – are of secondary
importance. Then you will no longer adhere to them, and
you open up for oneness with Brahman.

You should neither desire nor reject the joys of being. Enjoy
what is pleasant and accept with composure what is less
pleasant. Remember that all amusements are ephemeral. The
pleasant and the unpleasant will always alternate. Profit and
loss are coming and going in the external world. Those who
depend on amusements will always have to suffer. Those who
are connected with the everlasting bliss beyond duality will
stop desperately looking for worldly happiness.

To live in the world of form is a pleasure if there is a balance
between the inner dimensions of tranquility on the one hand
and the apparent external world on the other. Most people are
not aware of their inner dimension. This one-sidedness causes
their life to be largely trivial, uninspired and unsatisfactory.

14.   Peace arrives when the mind no longer adheres to external forms but reliably pursues its goal: oneness with Brahman.

Again and again we should be aware of inner peace and the completeness of the universe. This will gradually lead to a strong connection with our inner core of Being. The stronger this connection is, the more do the worldly ups and downs lose their hypnotic force.

Rejection and desire, complaining, being appalled and angry, and feeling sorry for ourselves are signs that we identify with thoughts and emotions. Recognize who you are and become free! Turning our consciousness toward the constant reality, toward Atman and Brahman, brings us liberation. That is how we break all chains created by our ego.

Acceptance is creating the connection with Being

15. Patience means confronting all of life's adversities without inner resistance, without anger and complaints.

The connection with Brahman comprises the absolute acceptance of Being as it presents itself. Non-acceptance means to reject life, the negation of life. Whatever confronts you, know that it is part of the divine Being.

The ego dissolves and the Atman can light up as soon as man confronts phenomena without superfluous desire and without emotional rejection. Again and again, the little ego likes to rebel against the Being as it presents itself. It always derives new energy from resisting what is. By restlessly striving for a change in its circumstances of life, the ego wishes to find fulfilment some time.

Rejecting the presence as it is, the ego is unable to enter the depth and fullness of Being. That is why it always only moves on life's surface. Yet in time, this surface is as barren and unfertile as a stony desert.

To accept "what is" does not mean leading a completely passive life. We accept what is because any other attitude would only mean conflict and a waste of energy. What is has already happened. In a state of composed and loving acceptance of what is, we can freely take the next step without fear, anger or selfish desire. That is how we change what can be changed! We leave behind what we can leave and want to leave!

We are making the best of every situation. In connection with our Self, we will creatively make the right moves. Acceptance of life as it is creates space for joy and love.

Inner resistance will only aggravate the problem. Anger, fury, fear and frustration result in reactions which usually increase the problem.

16. Always stay connected with your Atman, with pure consciousness; that is how you avoid mental unrest. React calmly to external happenings. Do not allow yourself to be consumed by sensory perception.

Viewed from a higher perspective, every moment is complete as it is, up to the smallest detail. Situations only become "terrible", "hopeless" or "unsatisfying" through our evaluation. Those who practice "non-evaluation" go beyond the dualist world of phenomena. They immerse in another dimension which contains neither "good" nor "bad". The grandeur of the universe reveals itself in connection with that dimension.

When we accept everything the way it is and stop to criticize, to condemn and to rebel against it, the "bad" will dissolve. It will lose its power for us personally and it will also affect others less negatively.

Again and again, even spiritually advanced people will feel angry when confronted with the ignorance and other weaknesses of others, or with their own shortcomings. That is truly no reason for to despair. We can always get off, take a step back from our mind, observe and accept even that aspect of "Being". Acceptance is a miracle cure leading to liberation.

Krishna: Those who remain serene in the face of pleasure and pain are truly wise and will achieve liberation.
Bhagavad Gita, 2:15

Identity – Who am I?

> 17. *Wishing for liberation means achieving one's own true nature. This happens through cutting the chains applied by egoism.*

Man begins to develop his ego consciousness in early childhood. His ability to think makes him feel like a person separated from the world. On the one hand, the ego is the main cause of suffering and strife, on the other hand it is the basis of all free individuality. For that reason, we should not condemn our own egotism and that of others, but see through its mission and thus reach a higher level of consciousness.

Plants and animals do not have the kind of ego humans have. They are still in a state of paradise, in oneness with God and the world.

Humans have left this oneness by their way of thinking. Jesus compared man with the "prodigal son" who left home to squander his inheritance (his original security and bliss) abroad (away from his origin). Nevertheless this son, when he finally returned, meant more to his father than the other son who had remained at home. The "prodigal son" had taken a developmental step which the other son did not take.

Through separation – caused by ego thinking – and the subsequent return to oneness, man achieved a higher consciousness. He is now not only one with God, but also a free individual. In Shankara's language, he is not only one with Brahman – as are stones, plants and animals – but he is also Atman, a liberated soul. That is the way in which pure consciousness can encounter itself. God encounters himself in His son, and the son encounters himself in his father.

*As sure as I am that I am human, I am sure that noth-
ing is as close to me as God. God is closer to me than
I am to myself; my Being depends on God being close
and present to me. He is as close to a stone and a
piece of wood, although they know nothing of it. If
the wood knew and could recognize how close God is
to it, as the highest angel knows, it would be just as
blessed as the highest angel. And that is why man is
more blessed than a piece of wood, because he recognizes God and knows how close God is to him.*

Meister Eckehart

*18.   Devotion is the direct way to liberation. In other
words, devotion means to find the sole reality of Atman.*

Every man is longing for liberation. Do not numb this longing through external deeds. Liberation can only be achieved
through devotion to the highest. Enquire in earnest for what
you really are. Give up your ego, your worries and fears, your
need to be important, your desire, your identification with the
physical and mental body.

Devotion is the equivalent of the tireless search for one's own
true nature. Again and again, it leads to the question: Who am I?

*19.   Man wants to find and understand himself. He
looks for his identity in the world of forms. But that can
never satisfy his longing.*

The ordinary man hardly thinks about his identity. Yet he has
a great need to be somebody special. Subconsciously he is busy
strengthening and defending his ego identity.

He identifies with:

- his body: "I am strong and young"; "I am beautiful and desirable" or "if only I were more attractive!" or "I am an old, sick person!"
- his feelings: "I am under stress" or "I am in love and the happiest man on earth!" or "I am afraid this or that might happen!"
- his intellectual concepts: "I am a Christian!" or "I am a victim of my upbringing!" or "Dangers are lurking everywhere!" or "I have achieved something in life!" or "I am a loser!"
- his past: "My name is Josef Brunner. I was born in Munich 42 years ago. Once I was best in class at school. I was married and am now divorced. I had to go through much";
- his present status: "I am unemployed, receiving social welfare!" or "I am a housewife" or "I am a successful businessman":
- his wishes, worries and hopes: "I will never be able to fulfill my dreams!" or "I hope I will meet my ideal partner" or "if only I had more money!"

Somebody could ask: "Why is it useful to come to terms with my identity? I simply am who I am!" Yes, it would be good have such carefree thoughts, but without noticing, we add a lot of attributes to this "I am who I am!" My name, my age, my past (as far as I remember it). These "stories" say little about my apparent personality and nothing at all about my inner identity.

You are not what you believe you are. And what you believe makes you unhappy in the long run. It creates problems and worries and makes you doubt whether your life has a purpose.

All the attributes of our "I am...", for example as enumerated above, were created by our thoughts. They constantly change, are fragmental and ephemeral. These attributes reduce the feeling of our Being to names, to limited intellectual concepts. They make us small, they impair our love for ourselves and thus also for the world.

At the end is death, of which normal man knows nothing either. By death we mean the passing of our body. If we identify with our body, this of course means a fear of inevitable aging and dying.

> *Find out: "Who am I?" The pure I is reality: absolute consciousness, absolute bliss. If we forget that, all the misery is revealed; if we keep that in mind, no misery will befall us.*
>
> Ramana Maharshi

Lost in thought

> *20. Man is lost in the sea of thought and feelings. He burns in the fire of painful comings and goings. He is tossed back and forth by unpredictable winds. Good and bad deeds of the past determine his karma. He is full of fear.*

Ordinary people do not realize that they are in a stream of thoughts all day long. They also do not know that they totally identify with the content of their thoughts. They are slaves and victims of their thoughts.

But our thoughts do not come very close to reality if at all. They consist of concepts we have been taught from childhood by parents, teachers, friends, society. In addition there are patterns which have been imprinted into our genes through the centuries and millennia by religions and collective thinking habits.

We look at the world from that vantage point. For as long as we are caught in those patterns, we "function" and "react", but we do not live the kind of life we could live.

The magic effect of our intellectual concepts makes us unhappy. For example, we believe sensational media reports showing that the world is bad, consisting primarily of misery and cruelty. We allow others to convince us that we are committing errors and sins.

Only when we again and again observe the thoughts and feelings constantly at work in our minds do we become aware of the patterns of our thinking, feeling and behaving, and we can finally liberate ourselves from these patterns.

21. Turn to the true masters, both the living and the dead. They have found peace and strength. It is their nature to support others. They have overcome the stormy sea of this world and are unselfishly helping to liberate others. As the moonlit night cools the earth when it is parched by the fiery rays of the sun, they show the way from confusion to inner peace.

Attachment and liberation

> *22.   The pupil asks:*
> *What does dependence mean? How does it come about?*
> *How can I be liberated from it? Please give me an*
> *answer!*

Dependence means to attach more value to ephemeral phenomena such as relationships and possessions, one's profession, success or failure, than to the origin of all Being, which is beyond the visible world. It is everlasting, full of joy, beauty and peace. To someone who has not experienced this transcendent world – Shankara calls it Atman and Brahman – the physical and mental existence feels difficult and problematic.

We can only live in the lightness of Being when we recognize the relative meaning of the external world. Then we can enjoy it as the game of Maya without depending on it. Then we must not fight for anything to be happy. We accept gladly what comes our way and don't miss what we don't have.

> *23.   The master speaks:*
> *No one is able to liberate others. The sick regain their*
> *health only when they take their medicine themselves*
> *and follow a diet. They do not become healthy through*
> *the effort of others.*

Everybody must take the only really important step in life himself. It consists of going beyond thinking and of connecting with the space beyond words. This is how we exceed the ego with its consciousness that is tied to the world of forms.

Primarily, our thinking is busy naming, analyzing, labelling and categorizing as bad or desirable the phenomena as we perceive them. This activity of the mind can be very useful for performing everyday tasks.

However, analytical thinking is unable to comprehend the phenomena in their entirety. It always remains at the surface of Being.

This becomes especially apparent when two people meet. We do not get to know the other by thinking and evaluating; we are primarily controlled just by our thinking patterns which we project upon the other. Our image of others usually mirrors our way of thinking. We only see how we think "about" the other without making any deeper spiritual connection. Often, it is only a few words we use to label a person: "He/she is dishonest!", or "He/she is an enemy!", "He/she is a friend!", "He/she is a good person/a bad person!"

24.   Reality will unveil itself only when we are prepared to see it. We all see the moon only with our own eyes. We can only cut our chains of uncertainty ourselves. Only we can liberate ourselves from the fruits of past labour.

Only in devotion and inner tranquility can we look behind the facade of phenomena and behind the veil of our evaluations.

When you are silent, you are what God was by nature and creature, of which He made your nature and creature.
When you are silent, you hear and see how God within you heard and saw before your own wanting, seeing and hearing began.

Jakob Boehme

25. *Education, articulate speech, prestige and exter-*
nal success may bring personal satisfaction. But they
won't bring liberation.

26. *Studying books of wisdom, all these efforts are*
useless as long as we do not experience Atman and
Brahman, the pure consciousness free of content.

27. *The jumble of knowledge and words resembles a*
dark, dense forest where thoughts wander about aim-
lessly. That is why a men of wisdom should earnestly
study the true nature of our Self.

There is an surplus of knowledge. Wisdom is a scarce commodity. Too much knowledge in the form of trivial TV information,
news items and such is blocking the way to Being.

"Know thyself!" is an age-old invitation to explore the meaning and the nature of our life. Why is it difficult to recognize
who we are? We are all placing too much power and trust in
our intellect. In spite of scientific progress, our intellect is very
limited. When it is honest, it can only tell us: "I know that I
know nothing!" Nothing has changed since Socrates coined
this phrase. We know precious little about the endless universe
with its hundreds of thousands of galaxies. Even the human
body and mind remains a great riddle in spite of all the scientific research. Why does our heart beat for a lifetime? How do
our cells grow and renew themselves? What is the vital force
in our body? How do thoughts and feelings evolve? Where do
they come from?

Knowledge is one part of life, wisdom is the other. Knowledge
can be useful, but also burdensome. Wisdom lets us recognize
what causes suffering and how we can liberate ourselves from
it. It leads to beauty and the fullness of life.

Thoughts and words are useful for helping us to orient ourselves in the world of forms. They are essential for communication. But we should also be aware that words are always just a weak reflection of reality. For example, we will never be able to describe the nature of a person with words. With words, we can only hint at reality. Words can be compared with a finger pointing to the moon. The finger is not the moon, but it can motivate us to perceive the moon.

Truth is our inner Self. Truth is the ever-present Being that unfolds from step to step and is everlasting because it is not subject to worldly comings and goings. Knowledge needs words. The truth of Being can only be found beyond words. The secret of Being reveals itself only in quiet loving devotion.

The only effective medicine

28.   There is only one medicine when the snake of ig-norance has bitten you. It is the achievement of Brah-man. Without that medicine, what use is the knowledge of the Vedas and other writings? Even miracle cures, trance, mantras, prayers and magical rituals cannot help you.

29.   A patient is not cured when he only pronounces the name of the medicine without taking it. It is useless to invoke your god without connecting with Brahman.

30.   You cannot achieve your true nature before liber-ating your consciousness from the world's illusion. Until then, declaiming the word "Brahman" only causes un-necessary noise.

31.   A treasure buried in the ground does not appear just because you call it. It requires good instructions. You have to dig, remove stones and such to get close to it. Just so, pure reality, hidden by the game of Maya, cannot be conjured up by mere wishing; it requires re-flection and meditation.

You are not liberated when you speak of God, but you are lacking the direct experience. That is only a waste of words. Only constant attention, contemplation and meditation will lead you to the clear light of consciousness.

32.   Therefore, the wise man should strive with all his might for liberation from attachments, just as a sick man will strive for health.

Non-adherence, composure and unselfishness

> *33.   The first step toward liberation consists of*
> - *Non-adherence to things, people, and all kinds of success;*
> - *Composure, patience, love of peace and self-control as described in the scriptures, determine the next step.*
> - *The third step is to give up deeds that serve to satisfy selfish desires.*

One of the fundamental problems that prevents love and causes suffering is adherence to things and persons. When something gives us joy, we want to hold on to it and repeat it. That is how adherence begins.

For example, when a man is in love with a woman, he wants to own her and bind her to him, to have her for himself. We are quickly fixated upon things and people we think we absolutely need to be happy. Unhappiness follows, whether we get what we want or not.

If we do not get what we desire, we are unsatisfied. Once we have what we want, we are in dread of routine or loss.

By desiring and adhering, we overlook the fullness and beauty of Being which always remain hidden.

We do not achieve liberation by giving up the joy of things or persons, by becoming an ascetic. It is not the joy of things or the relationship with a person that creates the problem, but the narrowing of our view, the urge to repeat, the idea that "I must have this for happiness!" or "I am suffering without ...!"

Adherence means that even when many requirements are met, one single unfulfilled requirement causes us to be plagued by a feeling of lack, of loss, of unfulfilled longing, and we are unhappy. There will always be something the mind is missing, wanting to have.

There is only one way to be liberated from adherence: composed observance of what is going on within us, what causes our adherence, how we are gripped and tortured by dependence. That is how we create distance, and desire dissolves.

As everyone knows from experience, it is usually quite useless to fight an addiction. It is no help to condemn or to chasten ourselves and at the same time to give free range to our wishes.

Better than desiring and rejecting is to develop a consciousness for everything that life is giving us every day , and to be grateful for it. Gratitude opens our eyes to the fullness and completeness of life.

Love and gratitude are one. When we love everything, when we "are" love, nothing can put us in chains. When we except nothing from our love, we do not adhere to one and reject or despise the other.

You may remain lovingly connected with what surrounds you in the world. Yet look at all external phenomena as a game of Maya, as things that come and go.

Those who are master of their senses will be without adherence and aversion. Those who look inward will achieve enlightenment. That ends all worries, and deep inner peace will follow.
Bhagavad Gita 2:64-65

Meditation is your true nature

34. The fourth, last and most important step is to en-
ter Atman through long-lasting meditation. This is how
wise men achieve their highest non-dualist state and
acquire the bliss of Nirvana.

To many people, meditation is something strange and difficult which they would rather do without. In contrast, the Indian wise man, Ramana Maharshi, declared: "*Meditation is your true nature! You call it meditation because other thoughts distract you. When these are no longer there, only you remain.*"

Meditation begins with attention. You meditate when you are aware of everything you perceive at the moment outside yourself and within yourself, without thinking about it. Through observation, obsessive thoughts lose their power and finally dissolve. What remains is a detached , liberating state of being aware.

Meditation is not only a technique that helps us to become more tranquil, to reflect, to restore calm, and at last to achieve liberation. Meditation, correctly understood, is a way of life.

Those who are mostly stressed all day long, get angry again and again about this and that, worry and chase after some ego goals, will make only modest progress with "sitting meditation" in the evening (from the Japanese zazen: za = to sit and zen = contemplation). Yet our everyday behaviour and meditation can fertilize each other. "Sitting" changes our daily life, and reversely the new quality of daily life has a strong effect on the depth of meditation.

Pay attention to how your daily life progresses, to what you want and what you do. Note whether you constantly get lost in unnecessary thoughts, and always return to the present moment. You can only really live in the "now" and open up for Being.

Largely, a "normal" person's thoughts wander around in the past or in the future. We can all quickly realize it when we observe our own constant stream of thoughts. We dwell within dead structures of thought, missing the depth and liveliness of present Being.

The shark of desire

35. The master speaks:
I will now explain the difference between Atman (pure
consciousness) and non-Atman (body, senses, mind).

36. Man's body consists of subtle and physical ele-
ments such as air, fire, water and earth. The different
combination and composition of these elements makes
up the physical body. It consists of substances such as
bone, flesh, blood and skin. These in turn form the head,
torso, arms and legs.

37. The five senses provide us with sound, touch,
sight, taste and smell. Our experiences originate from
these organs.

38. The consciousness of the ignorant depends on
ephemeral objects of experience. External things awak-
en desire. It is difficult to achieve liberation from these
bonds. That is why the ignorant are subject to their kar-
ma and have to be born again and again here and there.

39. The effect of external things is more dangerous
than the venom of the cobra, for these phenomena can
kill us by their mere appearance.

40. Knowledge of the sacred scriptures is useless
without dissolving the dependencies. Only those will
achieve liberation who have overcome the unfortunate
desire for material objects.

41. Those who are not free of longing cannot cross the sea of this world without suffering harm. The shark of desire will grab them by the throat and pull them under water.

42. Yet those who have killed the shark of desire for material objects with the sword of dispassion will cross the ocean of comings and goings without much difficulty.

43. Follow the way shown by the teachers of wisdom, and follow your own intuition. Practice the nourishing qualities of contentment, compassion, forgiveness, righteousness, tranquility and control. That is how you will harvest the fruits of wisdom.

The body – the instrument of experience

44.   The physical body is born from the karma of the previous life. It serves individuals as an instrument of experience. It helps a person to perceive material things. It serves as a temporary abode.

The body is a learning aid. It serves as a stage for the mind.

The body is also an important gate to man's essence. Superfluous thinking causes separation between mind and body. When we liberate ourselves from unnecessary thinking, when we are present, we can connect with the energy, the vital force and the endless wisdom of our body. With yoga, we consciously produce this connection. Observing our breathing and controlling our thoughts are the basis for penetrating the Being more deeply.

We often underestimate how important the body is for our spiritual development. The body not only serves us to experience the external world, but also to receive intellectual truths. Contemplation and meditation require a body as healthy as possible. Those who impair their body by lack of exercise, unhealthy and excessive food, nicotine or alcohol abuse, are limiting their access to reality. That is why we should endeavour a healthy life style.

The health of the body is determined mainly by mental nourishment. Thoughts cause feelings. They in turn are reflected in our body. All body cells react to feelings of joy as well as to feelings of anger and hatred, to worries and desires, etc. In the long run, negative thoughts lead to illness. Happy thoughts promote good health.

45.   Birth, blossoming, decay and death are the stages through which the body passes. It develops from childhood to adulthood. It suffers this or that illness.

The mental body

> 46. The inner nature of the body consists of four aspects:
>
> - The intellect (Manas). Closely connected with it are the emotions. Thinking causes analysis and the classification of perceptions.
> - Apart from the intellect, there is intuition (Buddhi). With it, we can recognize the real meaning of an object.
> - The inner core of the body also includes the ego (Ahamkara). It is caused when we identify with the body, our thoughts and feelings.
> - The fourth aspect is memory (Citta). It is like a huge warehouse preserving all our past thoughts, feelings, images and experiences.
>
> 47. The mental body (the mind), which is dominated by the external forms, is the reason why the soul must again and again experience the consequences of past deeds.

Depending on whether situations are regarded as pleasant or unpleasant, we experience desire or rejection. Our identification with the body, with thoughts and feelings, leads to the ego feeling. It forms an unreal I which hides our true nature.

The ego takes its identity mainly from the past. Usually we believe to be what we have experienced, what we have achieved, what has happened to us. We think we are our own history as we have preserved it in our memory: what we have suffered, what has gone good and wrong in our life.

When we are recognized and praised, the ego enjoys it. When we are disrespected, hurt, insulted, it reacts with disappointment, fury, self-pity and such.

Every characteristic, every role we play, every one of our "stories" from the past – they are not "we". We are what remains when all identification comes to an end.

"Citta" corresponds to the "subconscious" as it is used in psychology. The "subconscious" acts as a large storage tank in which all our memories are preserved. The patterns of thinking, feeling and acting in the "subconscious" determine our karma.

48. When we dream, the memories in the subconscious are activated, creating our own dream world. Our consciousness identifies with the images and events that occur not only in our dreams, but also when we are awake.

49. In dreamless sleep, the mental part of our body is turned off. Everyone can feel that in deep sleep, when the senses and the mind are at rest, we experience the bliss of Atman.

Why do we feel like born again after a healthy sleep? In our sleep, the incessant thinking that accompanies us throughout the day is interrupted. We do not think in deep sleep, and yet there is an "I" that remembers upon waking up: "It was good. I slept wonderfully well."

The energy and recreation we derive from deep sleep comes from the space beyond thoughts. Optimal regeneration is possible only in a state of non-thinking. In dreamless sleep, there are no objects of experience and no thoughts. In dreamless sleep, when we are free from these obstacles, we achieve the blessing of Atman.

Thinking is necessary and meaningful for some purposes, for example to analyze, plan and organize something. But to make good decisions, we need not only our intellect, but also the inner tranquility that allows us access to our intuition.

Nevertheless, about 90% of our daily thoughts are worthless repetition which only hinders us to confront the moment freely and easily. They are mainly occupied with subjects and conflicts from the past, and with wishes and worries about the future. These thoughts prevent us from being happy here and now.

50. The mental body is the tool for all actions of Atman. The Atman uses it as a carpenter uses an axe. Yet the Self always remains a pure consciousness. No karma, created by the shells surrounding it, can touch it.

51. The mind is a reflection of the light coming from Atman. The mind identifies with the body, with the perceptions, the thoughts and feelings. This identification causes the feeling of individuality.

The ego personality

> *52. The personal "I" is happy when its experiences are pleasant, and it suffers when they are unpleasant. Joy and pain belong to the ego personality. The Atman is not touched by it. It is always in a state of non-dualist bliss.*

The ego is caused by our mental separation from our original oneness. Without connection with its own essence and thus without access to universal consciousness, the "small I" feels like an incomplete and fragile being. Therefore the ego, usually subconsciously, is constantly trying to prove its special importance. It compares itself with others and suffers when it thinks to own less, to be less beautiful or less successful.

It takes every opportunity to inflate and to seek confirmation of its existence from others. To think and talk negatively about others gives it a feeling of "being" valuable itself.

When the little "I" thinks it does not do well in comparison with others, it tries at least to confirm its existence by feeling sorry for itself. It always finds external causes responsible for its misfortune. That is why some people like to tell how badly they are off, what illnesses they have, what they have had to endure, how mean others are …

The ego likes drama. It does not want life to be as simple as it actually is. With drama, it feels to be centre stage. It is important, it suffers, it struggles. It fights for its objects of desire, for its positions.

It considers it important to be smarter than others, to know everything better, to be in the right.

The ego is constantly busy overcoming problems which it has basically created itself. Subconsciously it loves all kinds of worries and problems. It derives its identity from these. It finds meaning in anxiety and struggle. If it were to recognize the beauty and lightness of Being, it would dissolve itself. That is not a reassuring prospect for the ego. It prefers to cope with a never-ending chain of difficulties. This process is accompanied by demands, envy, hatred, anxiety and worries. There is no end to this labour. There are always new things or events that bother the ego, and the ideal state it dreams of never becomes reality.

Even the effort to be "spiritual" can serve the ego. Some dream of enlightenment because they subconsciously hope to crown their "little I" with it.

53. The perceptions derived from the senses are not of importance to the sensory organs, but they serve the Atman. The Self is the greatest treasure of all and is always full of bliss. Only the ego causes and experiences suffering.

Maya, the great illusion

> *54. The goddess Maya symbolizes the power on which all phenomena are based. Maya gives birth to the entire universe.*
>
> *55. Maya is also called the great illusion. It has no beginning and works beyond all perception. It consists of the three Gunas. We can recognize the powers of Maya by wisely observing the Gunas.*

The universal consciousness, called God or Brahman, plays a strange game. It gives us the mind consisting of thoughts, feelings and memories. This mind gets lost in illusions through the influence of Maya.

We believe to perceive the world as it "really" is with our intellect in connection with our sensory organs. That is the great deception.

- We find this already from the fact that our sensory organs only perceive for what they are suited. A bat, for example, perceives the world very differently than man, through the ultrasound waves it emits and whose reflection it received. We only see a small section of the world.
- Our senses can distinguish solid, liquid and gaseous substances. As nuclear science confirms, all this material only consists of oscillations of energy, which is constantly changing. The forms come and go. That is the game of Maya.
- Of the hundreds of thousands of sensory impressions, we can register only what we are programmed for. In a street full of stores and displays, a women sees very different things than a man.

- Our mind immediately analyzes, labels and arranges every perception in our scheme of thinking and feeling. The mind functions according to its thinking, feeling and evaluation patterns. That is why we do not recognize the world as it is but how we evaluate it.
- Ordinary people only have access to the sensually perceivable world. They do not see the dimensions beyond the thoughts. This provides a very limited and distorted perspective, and that is the cause of their problems.

56. *Maya is neither Being nor non-Being, nor does she have part in either. She is neither divided nor undivided, nor a mixture of both. She is most wondrous. Her character is difficult to describe.*

57. *With the experience of Brahman, of the one without the second, we can see through the game of Maya.*

58. *The three Gunas, by which Maya reveals herself, are called Rajas, Tamas and Sattva. They have different characteristics.*

The powers of Maya work for the mind like a kaleidoscope, a pipe with several mirrors, through which the observer sees objects in many different patterns. The mirrors in the kaleidoscope can be compared with the three Gunas – Rajas, Tamas and Sattva. The three Gunas are the powers through which Maya works. The image of the world depends on how the gunas work together.

What we regard as the "objective world", resembles a mirage. The air is really mirrored, but it also conjures up something else. As everyone knows, we cannot quench our thirst in a mirage.

59. *The nature of Rajas is action. Through its power, the world begins to unfold. Rajas constantly produces dependence, desire and mental states such as sadness and suffering.*

60. *Rajas results in lust, fury, stinginess, pride, selfishness, avarice, envy, jealousy and other such weaknesses. They are characteristics connected with man's worldly tendencies. They mark the ego and are the cause for our involvement in the world of forms.*

Vigorous ego thinking causes strong emotions which promote rejection and desire. They in turn strengthen the emotions. This spiral results in desire, passion, hatred, avarice and suffering.

61. *Ignorance, inertia, stupidity and carelessness are the effects of Tamas. Those who are caught in them are in a state of trance, even while awake.*

62. *The power of Tamas will spread a veil over reality. It is the power of Tamas that makes things appear different than they are. Tamas gives Rajas a free range. Ignorance and dullness are also the cause for repeated transmigration.*

Even though all our actions belong to Maya's illusion, they are not meaningless for the dualist level either. They are subject to the law of cause and effect that can be observed everywhere in the world of forms. They subsequently cause our karma. It means that good deeds lead to good destiny. Likewise, selfish, unloving deeds come back to haunt the doer.

63. Even clever and learned men are overcome by dullness. They do not understand the Atman. They regard their deceptions as true and let themselves be misled by them. The unhappy effect of Tamas is indeed powerful!

The mind creates the problems

64. Confusion and a lack of judgment accompany those who are caught in illusion. They are plagued by doubts. They are constantly involved in difficulties caused by their own projections.

Those unawakened believe that their difficulties exist objectively outside themselves. If they look closely, they recognize that they are all projection of their own mind.

There are no difficulties in total presence. We can all find this immediately by checking: "What problem do I have NOW at this moment?!" In total presence, when we do not think of yesterday or tomorrow, we are without problems and worries. There may be tasks and challenges to deal with. They can be handled "step by step", and always only "here and now". When we separate from the intellect that causes the problems, the dimension beyond the Maya will always give us the right intuition to meet the tasks of the external world.

Inner conflicts are caused especially by evaluating situations, for example by thoughts such as: "This is terrible!" or "This should not be!" or "How am I going to do it? It is so difficult!"

Those who master their thoughts will examine: "What am I to do, and how can I do it?" If he is so inclined, he will go and meet the requirements. He will always trust the completeness of Being, no matter what happens. He will always trust that "fate will make no mistake!".

Jesus: Are not two sparrows sold for a penny? And not one of them will fall to the ground apart from your father. But even the hairs of your head are all numbered. Fear not therefore: You are of more value than many sparrows.
Matthew 10:29-31

Sattva, the mirror of Atman

65.   The pure Sattva is clear as water. Yet clouded by Rajas and Tamas, it still leads to transmigration. The pure Sattva mirrors the nature of Atman as the sun illuminates the whole world.

66.   Sattva occurs as compassion, modesty, control, love of truth, trust, devotion and longing for liberation. Sattva causes spiritual tendencies and separation from attachment.

67.   The signs of pure Sattva are cheerfulness, the achievement of one's own Self, greatest peace, harmony, satisfaction and constant devotion to Atman.

Our thinking limits our identity to a very small, insignificant, ephemeral, fearful and yet somehow important person. Deep within us, we all suspect the immeasurable and inexhaustible vastness of existence. We all carry within us the strong urge to recognize and to live what we really are.

The universe does not leave us alone with our difficulties and with the confusion caused by Maya. We are not helplessly at the mercy of Rajas and Tamas. Through Sattva (insight, clarity, intuition) we always have an opportunity to cut the chains of the ego and of Maya.

68.   We recognize the body, the vital energies, the senses, the thinking and feeling, the ego and all the forms and objects of perception. But all that is not the true nature of man. All these life forms are ephemeral.

The forms of the world are not separate from Brahman. They reflect, more or less clearly visible to us, the beauty and the joy of pure consciousness. We can recognize this particularly well in nature, in crystals and flowers, trees or animals. Even small children show how connected they still are with the lightness of Being. Yet as man grows up, he becomes more and more involved in his thinking, in his problems, and he loses the innocence of childhood. Through confused thinking, a lack of trust in Being, through anxieties and worries, he hardens more and more. That is why the core of his being, the Atman, has difficulty shining through his external shells.

This stiffening, caused by the magic impression of external phenomena, should be reversed again. As Jesus said: *"Truly I say unto you: Unless you change and become like little children, you will never enter the kingdom of heaven."* (Matthew 18:3).

Without having to forego our intelligence and life experience, we can experience a day like a child happy about the first snow of winter, catching snow flakes falling from the sky and looking at them in wonder. We can devote ourselves to the moment like a child blowing dandelion seeds into the wide world. We can open our hearts wide every day to absorb what the new day will give us. We don't have to continue living as we have done until now. Every day offers us thousands of opportunities to participate in the wonderful game of life with joy.

The condition is our ability to stop our intellectual and analytical, purpose-oriented thinking when we do not need it.

The Atman is eternal conscious Being

> 69.   The master speaks:
> *I will now reveal to you the nature of the highest Self,*
> *the pure consciousness. When you achieve it, you will*
> *be free from your chains and will reach fulfilment.*

The question about one's own identity cannot be answered with our limited intellect. As indicated, our thoughts can only provide inadequate information about this. The true everlasting Self can only be found in the depth of Being, in the silence beyond words.

We all can connect with our Atman, which is pure consciousness with all content removed. We don't have to be a scholar for this, or particularly intelligent. Trust your inner voice! That is how you will safely reach the goal.

The way to the goal is not a real way, and the goal is not a real goal. What you are yearning for deep within you IS YOU. You are nothing but the Atman. You have to do nothing to be what you are. You must only give up what you are not.

> *Thou needst not cry to God,*
> *The spring wells up in thee.*
> *Don't stop its fountain head*
> *It flows eternally.*
>
> Angelus Silesius

> 70.   *The Atman is the absolute truth, the essence of*
> *consciousness. It is a self-emerging truth without begin-*
> *ning and without time. It forms the foundation of our*
> *"I" consciousness. It is spectator to the activities of the*
> *body, the sensory organs and our vital energy. It ob-*
> *serves the movements of the mind.*

> *71.   The Atman is witness to all that happens while we are awake, in dreams and in deep sleep.*

It helps us to awaken from the illusion of forms when we realize as often as possible: "*I am not the perceptions, I am not the thoughts, the feelings! I am the observer!*" Always connect in your consciousness with the "observer" of events around and within you! Distinguish between the observer and the contents of the observation!

The observer is and always was present. All memories are possible only because their contents were recorded by the observer. Yet ordinary people do not perceive the observer, their own Self, because they lose themselves in the contents of their observation.

> *72.   The Atman is pure conscious Being. Atman can observe everything but cannot be viewed by anyone but itself. The Atman constitutes and brightens the power of recognition without requiring an external light.*

> *73.   The world of phenomena is permeated by its reality. It is ablaze with the reflection of its light.*

We should not underestimate or even despise the world of phenomena. Only when we include in our perceptions the light, the spirit behind the forms, can we correctly appreciate the ephemeral. Only then do we recognize the value and meaning of forms. Only then can we enjoy them without depending on them.

> *74.   The Atman animates all the cells and functions of the body. It enables our thinking, feeling, wanting.*

75. *Its nature is eternal conscious Being. All phenomena can be traced back to it.*

76. *The Atman is the innermost Self. Its essence is everlasting bliss. It is unchangeable, pure consciousness. It controls all functions of the body.*

77. *The light of Atman works in the body and illuminates the spirit of Sattva. It inspires thinking. It provides the whole universe with its splendour.*

Most people do not trust their own Self. They do not trust the wisdom and completeness of Being. That is why they are (usually subconsciously) afraid not to have enough strength and good fortune to successfully complete their tasks.

In the area of external forms, negative thoughts have dire consequences. They weaken our mental forces. We call it the law of resonance, which states that fear attracts what is feared. Likewise, distrust leads to disappointment. Unkindness and aggressiveness will lead to conflicts. Trusting in life brings us fullness on our way. Those who radiate love will meet with love. Beauty in the heart will make us experience the world's beauty.

Therefore it is important to connect mentally with the completeness of being – every evening, every morning, and before every task. Only thus can we be on our way with lightness, happiness and success. Thus we ourselves become a source of joy and confidence for others.

78. *The Atman controls the body's vital functions. It is the source of the mind. It is the basis of ego-thinking. Yet it is not influenced in the least by the body, the mind or the ego.*

79.   It is neither born nor does it die. It neither grows nor decays. Just as the air in a vessel that is broken does not cease to exist, the Atman is untouched by the death of the body.

80.   The Atman illuminates everything, the real and the unreal, without changing itself. It acts in all states of consciousness as the basic feeling: "I am". It is witness to all that happens.

The cleansing of thoughts

> *81. By cleansing and mastering our thoughts and feelings, we can directly experience the Self within us. This is how we cross the boundless sea of coming and going, whose waves are birth and death, joy and sorrow. Blessed are those who thus experience their own essence as identical to Brahman.*

The mind is tortured by impatience, anger, desire, worries and fears. Those emotions, anchored deeply within us, cannot simply be discarded. There is also no point in fighting them, as they would only gain strength. The result would be feelings of guilt and failure. We cannot force ourselves to be good and loving, and this is not necessary. At the depth of our soul, we all ARE complete and loving beings.

Only light can drive away darkness. Becoming conscious is our only salvation! Subconscious emotions determine whether you are well or unwell. Learn again and again, at every opportunity, to observe your emotions carefully and attentively without judging them as good or bad. That is when weaknesses like hurt, self-pity, desperation, resentment, fury, anger, jealousy or desire will dissolve by themselves.

Ignorance hides the Self

82.   Through ignorance we identify with our body, and we constantly try to delight it with pleasant things and experiences. By identifying with things which are not the Self, we create bondage. Material objects bind us like the thread that binds the caterpillar to the cocoon. The result is a cycle of birth and death.

83.   Those who are marked by ignorance will value things wrongly. They mistake a snake for a rope. This brings them in great danger. They mistake ephemeral forms for reality and are therefore chained by them.

84.   The Self is invisible, eternal and the only reality. Ignorance hides the Self just as the sun darkens when the moon moves in front of it.

85.   When the Atman with its pure power of brightness is hidden, we begin to identify with the non-Self. Then Rajas unfolds its strength. Deceptive forms of thoughts and feelings are projected on the screen of Self. This results in the chains of desire, anger and other passions.

Samsara, the cycle of coming and going

> *86.   When a man is devoured by the great shark of ig-*
> *norance, he drifts up and down in the boundless ocean*
> *of Samsara. What a sad fate!*

The Sanskrit term "Samsara" means "constant wandering". In Hindu and Buddhist tradition, the soul must take part in the cycle of rebirth until it liberates itself from involvement in the external world and becomes one with its true Self.

In a certain sense, every waking up in the morning is a kind of reincarnation. We slide back into our body, we reactivate our patterns of thought, feeling and behaviour. We reactivate the old karma and establish it anew. We can only leave this hamster wheel through careful observation of our inner pattern.

> *87.   As the sun is hidden by clouds which it created*
> *itself with its rays, the ego consciousness created by the*
> *force of Maya is hiding the original Self.*

> *88.   When the Atman is no longer present due to igno-*
> *rance, this is like a day of bad weather when the sun is*
> *hidden by thick clouds, and stormy winds are blowing.*
> *Man is tossed about by heavy turbulence like a cloud.*

You are Sat-Chit-Ananda

89.   Dependence on the non-Self arises from ignorance which is without beginning and without end. It leads to the long sequence of birth, growing up, illness, invalidity and death.

90.   This attachement cannot be destroyed with weapons, storm or fire, and not with millions of deeds. Only the wonderful sword of recognition about the ephemeral and the everlasting will bring salvation. That sword is a gift of Brahman.

Attachement is caused mainly when we reject the "now" as it is. With our sensory organs, we constantly experience things which our thinking then interprets either as good and bad or as pleasant and unpleasant. We adhere to pleasant experiences and reject the unpleasant. Our ego forces us to say: "I like this!" or "I don't like this". But the ego is not satisfied with that. Confused by Tamas and encouraged by Rajas, the ego is again and again looking for things, people and events it might like, engaging in a never-ending struggle to escape unpleasantness. Thus we constantly chase after some wishes, hopes and goals.

Tamas ensures that the external forms are not recognized as a game of the divine Maya. Situations we encounter are as they are. If we can confront them without rejection or adherence, we remain free and form no new karma.

All new conflicts result from unnecessary evaluation and rejection. Those who can accept with composure the Being as it presents itself at present, has no psychological difficulties. There may be this or that to do, but that is no problem for the liberated "I". Why turn a situation into a drama? To those who are connected with the Atman, all existing problems virtually solve themselves. They take pleasure in devoting themselves to a task that gives them life and brings them joy.

91.   When the identification with the body, the thoughts and all other forms is dissolved, the Atman reveals itself in its pure essence as unclouded and eternal bliss.

92.   By distinguishing between the true Self and the non-Self, we achieve full enjoyment. We recognize ourselves as Sat-Chit-Ananda (Being, consciousness and bliss).

Sat-Chit-Ananda is the "description" of the actual "indescrible" Brahman. As the old Indian scriptures indicate, Brahman is without attributes. As long as man "remembers" his oneness with Brahman, he enjoys "Being, consciousness and bliss".

93.   Those who recognize their true nature as untouched by all the happenings will be free and will rest in themselves.

The body is ephemeral

*94.	The nature of the body is ephemeral. Its "life" is only a reflection of Atman. You can observe the body, but you are not the body.*

*95.	The human body lives on nourishment and dies without it. It is an assembly of different substances and therefore cannot be the eternal, pure Atman who exists on its own.*

*96.	The body appears on earth only for a short time. It exists neither before its birth nor after its death. Its abilities are ephemeral, and it changes constantly. It can be an object for observation. Therefore it cannot be the own Self which is witness to all ephemeral forms.*

*97.	The body consists of different parts such as torso, arms and legs. It can continue to live when various parts of it are lost. It is determined by outside forces and therefore cannot play an independent role. It therefore cannot be the Self.*

The uninvolved witness

> 98. The Atman as the eternally remaining reality dif-
> fers from the body, from its activities, its characteristics
> and states. It is the witness and observer. This is be-
> yond doubt.

In the pure awareness we encounter the Self. We are not the
body. We are not even "our thoughts", "our feelings" and not
"our deeds". Those are only the ephemeral expressions of
Maya. But they also belong to the universal consciousness
as we do ourselves and everything else in the spiritual and
physical world.

We are the uninvolved witness of all phenomena. We are not
the ephemeral events, but the observer.

When all identification of the consciousness with something
ends, only the observer remains. The observer has no content,
he is not this or that, but the one who perceives the contents.

To the observer, life never becomes boring. He sees not only
the surface of phenomena, but also the space, the dimensions
behind them.

The observer sees movements of the mind, the thoughts and
the feelings. They change only because he observes them.
Negative thoughts and feelings dissolve.

The observer is your eternal core of Being, your greatest joy
and love. This is how those who become aware of themselves
give gifts to themselves and to the world.

Do not worry! The uninvolved witness does not stop having
human feelings, but these feelings take on a different quality.
He is no longer involved in the suffering resulting from his own
ego and from that of others. He can enjoy all small and great

beauties of the world, but he is no longer addicted and servile to persons, things and events. He is able to feel great compassion, but he does not suffer as others do.

99. The fool thinks "I am the body", the scholar thinks "I am the body and the soul". The wise man, on the other hand, has come to recognize by distinction: "I am Brahman".

100. Identification with ephemeral forms alone is the root of suffering. This root must be destroyed. When erroneous identification has been removed, all suffering ends.

The mind can bind and free us

101. The mind, together with the organs of perception, forms a shell around the Atman. This produces the feeling of "I" and "mine".

102. The mind is very effective. It distinguishes perceived things and gives them names.

103. Ignorance evolves in the mind. Thinking is very limited. Ignorance is the cause for the connection with comings and goings.

104. When thinking predominates, the world of forms evolves. On the other hand, when man goes beyond thinking, inspired by Atman, the illusion of the world dissolves for him.

Collective patterns of thought determine how nations and cultures think. This causes individuals to be convinced that their thinking must be correct. Yet in fact, most people are farther away than ever from the reality of being because their thinking is shaped by the world of forms.

105. In a dream, when there is no connection with the outside world, it is only the mind that creates all phenomena. Being "normal" awake is like an extended dream, there is no difference. The universe is only a projection of the intellect.

106. In dreamless sleep, when the mind is not active, nothing exists, as we all experience. Therefore man, who is subject to birth and death, is only a creation of his senses. He has no objective reality.

107. *The wind brings clouds and drives them away again. In the same way, man's attachment is caused by the mind, which can also dissolve it again.*

108. *The mind causes the soul to be chained to the body and to material objects. It binds man the way an animal is held by a rope. But thinking can cut the chains by ending the desire for material objects.*

109. *The mind is the cause of the chains as well as the instrument of liberation. Caught by Rajas man finds himself chained. Cleansed of desire and ignorance, the mind will lead to liberation.*

110. *Therefore those who want liberation should have their mind cleansed by distinction and letting go.*

111. *The mind produces innumerable sensory experiences. It causes all the different social positions, actions and their effects.*

112. *The mind obscures the originally pure consciousness, binds it with the chains of the body and the senses. It produces ideas of "I" and "mine" and always demands new entertainments.*

113. *The mind constantly adds new contents to the nature of the ego. People dominated by Rajas and Tamas are always eager for new experiences.*

It is wonderful to learn in the external world, to have new experiences, to extend one's knowledge, to unfold one's talents.

We only come in conflict when we are not in connection with our true Self. Then our efforts are lacking orientation, and too easily are we lost in the dramas of our ego. As a wheel cannot function without its hub, we are lost in the labyrinth of external forms without reference to our Self.

114. The wise men have recognized the mind as the origin of the ignorance by which all phenomena are moved just as masses of clouds are moved by the wind.

115. Therefore the seeker for liberation must carefully cleanse the mind. Then he will easily harvest the bliss of connection with the Self.

Thoughts and feelings are just as ephemeral as all other forms of this world. They constantly cause noise within us.

There is only one way to overcome the suffering of this world: to end useless thoughts which constantly circle around our desires and difficulties. Become an observer of your thoughts and feelings! Turn toward the powerful silence beyond the noise of thoughts. That is how the chains of your consciousness are cut. That is how the "I", which was lost to the world, finds back to itself.

When thinking is turned off, space is created for our real Being, space for love beyond worries, desire and rejection. Basically, all people yearn for this other dimension, for Being without thinking. People consume drugs such as alcohol, nicotine or cannabis because of that yearning. Drugs will temporarily dampen thought and cause a feeling of well-being. Apart from causing damage to health, they strengthen the attachment to material things. An addiction to watch TV and similarly numbing entertainments subconsciously serves the purpose of displacing bothersome thinking.

To open ourselves to the lightness of being that we know from the days of our childhood, we must awaken from our obsessive, incessant, uncontrolled thinking. Thought is a wonderful tool for communicating with the world. It helps us to fulfill our duties. But even for that, we also need "non-thinking". Wise decisions in harmony with the whole can only come from the space beyond thought. That is the space of unlimited opportunities, the only space in which the new, the creative, the progressive can be born.

116. Those who concentrate on liberation from all attachment to material objects will forget all deeds and immerse themselves in the reality of Brahman by means of regular exercises.

117. The mind cannot be the true Self because it is changeable, it has a beginning and an end. It is the cause of all suffering and can be observed like every other object. The observer himself differs from the contents of the mind.

The shell of the intellect

118. The intellect is the cause of identification, which in turn causes the cycle of birth and death.

119. The intellect is a reflection of pure consciousness. However, it identifies with the body and its abilities.

120. The intellect has no beginning. It causes the ego feeling and originates all activities in the relative world. It generates good and bad deeds and is responsible for their consequences. It causes pleasure and suffering.

121. The intellect is very strong and convincing due to its relationship with the true Self. It connects consciousness with the body, the circumstances of life, the past and present actions. Thus the ego consciousness is formed with its karma.

122. The Atman, which is pure wisdom, radiates into our heart. While the Atman is unchangeable itself, we become "actors" and "discoverers" when we identify with the mind.

In the apparent world, we are the "actors", subject to the law of karma. We are the "actors" as long as we identify with our body and the content of our thoughts and our will. Yet the "actor" and the "karma" dissolve when we see through Maya and end our identification with the "Non-Atman".

123. The Atman is beyond the limits of the intellect. However, man can identify with the movements of the mind.

124. Thanks to this connection with the unreal, it looks as if the Self, although unchangeable, has taken on the character of the mind. It resembles the fire that seems to assume the properties of a red-hot iron.

125. The Self's illusion of identity with thoughts and forms exists as long as the true nature of Atman is not recognized. When we mistake a rope for a snake, the deception ends as soon as we examine the matter more closely.

126. The illusion ends when we clearly distinguish between what really constitutes the Self and what doesn't. This happens when we experience the identity of our own soul with Brahman, when the deception ends like a dream upon awakening.

127. Soiled water becomes clean again when the mud is removed. In the same way, the true lustre of Atman reappears when the unreal is removed. When selfishness is ended, the individual soul reveals itself as Atman.

The shell of external happiness

128. *The shell of external happiness is also a manifestation of Maya. It reflects the bliss of Atman. Within this shell we experience the joys caused by objects we regard as pleasurable. This includes the fruits of our good deeds.*

129. *We experience the bliss of Atman during deep sleep. On the other hand, the non-liberated will experience it while dreaming or being awake only when pleasant things happen.*

130. *The shell of external happiness is not the highest Self. It has variable properties and is affected by Maya. It is promoted by good deeds. Yet everlasting and independent pleasure is achieved only in the fulfilment of Atman.*

Krishna: All beauty, all the magnificent creations of this universe come from my power.

Bhagavad Gita 10:41

131. *The pupil: If all shells such as the body, the mind, etc. are recognized as unreal and are abandoned, nothing remains but emptiness, the absence of everything. With what can a seeker of Self identify?*

132. *The master replies:*
That is a good question! It is the Atman through which all phenomena and also the ego will be recognized. However, the Atman itself is usually not observed. The Atman can only be recognized through the acuity of distinction.

133. The Atman cannot be observed by anyone other than himself. Self-recognition means perceiving Atman through oneself.

Only the Atman can perceive the Atman – who else? When consciousness encounters itself, creation goes beyond the bare consciousness that animals and ordinary people have.

134. Recognize the Atman, your true Self, in your heart. It is the witness of your ego and the workings of your mind. It is experienced as Being, consciousness and bliss.

135. The fool thinks the reflection of the sun he sees in a pail of water is the sun itself. It is the same kind of foolishness to identify with the reflection of consciousness in the mind. The wise man ignores the sun's reflection and knows that the sun provides all creatures with its rays while it is independent of them.

136. The body and the mind, in which consciousness is reflected, should be regarded in the same way. That is how we recognize our true Self as witness to all happenings, as the pure consciousness without any attributes, as everlasting and omnipresent. When we achieve that, we will be free of sin, suffering and death. We will become the epitome of joy.

137. There is no other way to break the chains of ephemeral existence than to achieve one's own true nature.

Brahman – the One without a second

138. Recognition that our own identity is inseparable from Brahman means liberation from the cycle of re-births. Recognize that Brahman alone is real!

Jesus: Whoever hears my word and believes him who sent me has eternal life and will not be judged but has crossed over from the dead to the living.

John 5:24

The dead of whom Jesus speaks correspond to those caught in the illusion of Maya. They are subjected to the "karma judgment". They must bear the consequences of their actions in this life and in the next lives. Yet those who can distinguish the ephemeral from the everlasting, who recognize their identity with Brahman, are free from Samsara (the wheel of rebirth); they have "crossed over from the dead to the living".

139. The diversity of forms we experience is nothing but Brahman, the One without a second. The absolute is free from all the restrictions of the human intellect.

140. The whole universe has evolved only from Brahman and has no independent existence.

141. Sri Krishna, who knows all secrets, explains in the Bhagavad Gita: "All beings dwell within me, but I am not in them." (Gita 9:4-5).

142. Thus the world does not exist in separation from Brahman. There is no reality to what our mind figures out in contrast. Every separation from Brahman is a deception.

143. Whatever we perceive, it is always Brahman, and whatever else is added to God is nothing but names.

Maya is a child of Brahman. Maya shapes the world with its happenings. Brahman reveals himself in these, but he himself is beyond any contents that could be described with pictures or words.

Thus God reveals himself to Moses as he approaches the burning bush (Exodus 3:14), asking for the name of God: "*I am that I am*". God (Brahman) has no name. God is not a person. He is the all-encompassing Being. Every content, every name would be a limitation. Brahman is consciousness without any conceivable contents, simple pure Being. Yet within, he bears all possibilities of external forms.

We use the "name" of God or Brahman to communicate with each other. Shankara speaks about the characteristics of the all-encompassing God. He indicates the unspeakable. Yet in the end, only experiencing the nameless is of any value.

144. Thus only Brahman alone exists, the One without a second. He is pure consciousness, flawless, the essence of wisdom and peace itself. He is timeless and beyond all activity. He represents absolute bliss.

145. His nature is invisible, immeasurable, formless, nameless, indestructible, beyond all suffering, and radiant from within. He comprises all diversities brought out by Maya.

146. The visionaries recognize Brahman as the knower, the knowledge and the known.

147. Brahman can neither be left nor reached. He is beyond thoughts and words, immeasurable, all-encompassing, without beginning and without end. He is the greatest splendour.

Naught ever can be known in God: He is a unique One. To know Him, Knower must be one with Known.
Angelus Silesius

148. The sacred scriptures confirm the absolute identity of Brahman and Atman, using the often repeated words: "Tat-Tvam-Asi" (This is You). This identity is difficult to comprehend because the terms Brahman and Atman seem to have different meanings, as the sun and the glow worm or the king and the servant, the sea and a well, or Mount Meru and the atom.

149. Yet these differences are only of the intellectual kind. In reality they are the effect of Maya. When we remove the projections, there is neither a supreme God nor an individual soul. A king is defined by his kingdom, a warrior by his weapons. Taking those away, there is neither a king nor a warrior.

The Atman in its essence is identical to the universal consciousness. However, it is not without peculiarity and individuality. It comprises the essence of all the experiences that have ever been lived. Yet this sum is without concrete contents. This essence cannot be described with words. It can be compared approximately to the "I" feeling we had in deep sleep without thoughts or images and which we remembered when we woke up.

Through enlightenment, the ego dissolves, but the individual pure consciousness remains. It is not – as some philosophers think – that "enlightenment" means to extinguish individuality.

In that case, who would ever achieve and experience enlightenment? Who enters the state of highest liberation? What point would there be for man's way from the original paradise to segregation only to overcome that separation? This is the way that has enabled man to achieve an individuality, his own centre of consciousness.

In Brahman there is diversity in oneness and oneness in diversity. The countless humans and their Atman can be compared with the trillions of cells in a body. As science has discovered, no cell is identical to another. Each cell leads a separate life. And yet, no single cell exists apart from the body. Each cell is one with the body, and yet it is unique. It has its own life in a community, it has individuality and is yet part of the whole. Each cell is carried and energized by the same vitality that determines all life.

The difference between the "individuality" of the body cells and the individuality of man lies in man's ability to self-reflect and thus to perceive his Self.

150. Brahman is "neither this nor that". It means that Brahman or Atman cannot be described with any intellectual content. That is the only way in which we can understand the oneness of the two.

151. The meaning of the two terms, Brahman (universal being) and Atman (individual Being) must be considered carefully. Neither the rejection nor the affirmation of their oneness leads to the truth.

Atman is Brahman, and Brahman is Atman. This is a contradiction only for the ordinary intellect. Logically, we say: If A equals B, and B equals A, then A and B must be identical. Yet according to Shankara's teaching, they are identical and also different. That is the peace and the wisdom of God.

> 152. Brahman and Atman share the same essence, namely pure consciousness. In that sense there is no difference between them.

There is only the one Being, in which not only Brahman rules, but in which there is also room for the diversity of forms and the diversity of all Atmans. All is Brahman, and Brahman is all. However, the human intellect finds it difficult to united diversity and oneness.

> 153. Atman is self-existent and as free as the sky. It cannot be described with words. Cleanse your mind, and then you will recognize your true "I" as absolute consciousness.

> 154. All objects made of clay, such as a jug, will always just have that clay as their basic substance. In the same way, the entire universe, which originates with Brahman, is only Brahman, the only truth, and nothing else. Therefore, our Self is also only cheerful, pure and supreme Being.

> 155. Just as places, time, objects and people are unreal in our dreams, so is the world, as we experience it when we are awake, only a product of our ignorance. The body, its organs, our breath and our imagined "I" are equally unreal. They are nothing but pure, blessed and supreme Brahman.

> 156. What is mistakenly regarded as a separate existence proves to be one with Brahman when the truth is recognized. The diverse world dissolves like a dream when we wake up.

This is you!

157. Everything beyond castes, religion, origin and family, everything free of names and forms, of awards and guilt, everything beyond space and time and all material objects – that is Brahman, and that is you. Meditate about it!

158. The highest reality beyond all words, yet accessible with the clear eye of insight, the pure consciousness, that is you. Meditate about it!

159. You are Brahman. You are untouched by the six weaknesses: hunger and thirst, decay and death, desire and ignorance. You find yourself in the heart of the yogis who meditate about you. You cannot be comprehended by the senses or the intellect.

160. Brahman is the foundation of the diverse phenomena of the universe. But they are all products of Maya. You are independent in your existence. This is you! Mediate about it!

161. You are free of birth, growth, development, decay and death; nothing can destroy you; you are the fundamental basis of creation, preservation and dissolution of everything. Meditate about it!

162. You are free of differences, immovable as an ocean without waves. You are freedom without end. Open yourself for that!

163. Although you are the One without the second, you are the cause of diversity.

164. There is no duality within you. You are endless and indestructible, your Being is beyond Maya. You are flawless, continuous bliss.

165. Although you appear with different names in different shapes, as gold comes in different forms, you always remain unchanged.

166. All is Brahman. There is nothing outside that Being.

167. Meditate about those truths of Brahman. Without a doubt you will arrive at a wisdom as pure as the water in your hand.

168. Brahman is beauty and love. You will find Brahman, the absolute existence, deep within your own heart.

Many believe that love is a rare commodity. They yearn for love, they think they must make great efforts to receive love, or that "great love" is a stroke of luck, similar to a win in a lottery.

In reality, the entire visible universe consists only of love. Even though it may appear otherwise: You are love, everything is love. We cannot even escape love. This cannot be proven, but it needs no proof, it is obvious. Or can anyone doubt that our wonderful, unbelievably beautiful world, the mountains and valleys, the flowers and trees, the creeks and rivers and lakes and oceans, the clouds and winds and seasons, the animals and humans, were born of anything but endless wisdom, beauty and love? How can anything in this world not be love? Only the aberrant mind creates darkness. But it has no reality. Darkness dissolves in the light of recognition.

> *If the sun were not love, its beauty would have no light.*
> *If the earth and the mountains were not love,*
> *no grass would grow on them.*
>
> *Jalal Al-din Rumi*

Even though the truth has been recognized, the impression often remains that we are acting and experiencing. This is leading to rebirth. This illusion must be carefully avoided by staying in constant connection with Brahman.

We do not accomplish anything alone in this world. You cannot even move your body without using the body's intelligence, its nerves and muscles. Thus all that happens on earth is interconnected. Nothing happens outside the all-encompassing Being. Everything is a game of Maya. IT thinks, IT acts, IT happens. Forget your "I", become a witness of the happening!

169. Stop identifying with the "I" and the "mine"! Recognize your inner Self, the Atman, the witness to happenings within you and outside you.

170. Forget all traditions! Liberate yourself even from the teaching in the scriptures. Just follow your pure inner voice!

171. The fragrance of sandalwood reappears when it is cleansed of all dirt. So does the fragrance of the supreme Self reappear when it is cleansed of the endless aberrations of the mind. It will reveal itself again as the supreme truth.

172. The more the mind becomes acquainted with the absolute, the less it depends on external experiences.

173. *Tamas is overcome by Rajas as well as by Sattva. Rajas dissolves itself through Sattva. In the end, the latter is also discontinued when the light of the Atman radiates.*

174. *It could be that old conditioning remains effective longer in the mind. Do not be distracted by that but follow your path with patience.*

175. *Be aware of this: "I am not the I that depends on the body but the supreme reality called Atman or Brahman!" Forget all other attributes!*

176. *The wise man does not care about acquisition or loss, for he neither wishes for anything nor does he reject anything.*

Jesus: Look at the birds of the air; they do not sow or reap or store away in barns, and yet your heavenly Father feeds them. Are you not much more valuable than they?
But seek first his kingdom and his righteousness, and all these things will be given to you as well.
Matthew 6:26-33

177. *For those with recognition, the world is only am ephemeral image that appears in the mirror Brahman.*

178. *As an actor takes off his mask, so does the wise man end his identification with unreal things.*

Like actors, we have to play many different roles in the external world. We are child, mother or father, pupil, breadwinner, etc.

In the world of appearances, do not shirk your responsibilities, but do play your role like an actor! Perform your duties, but do not identify with them! Then it becomes a heavenly game, and you can enhance his game with your joy, love and wisdom.

179. This external universe is completely unreal. Even the "I" has no reality, for it is ephemeral.

180. The real self is witness to the ego and its surroundings. This witness is omnipresent, even when you are in a state of deep sleep. This observer of all changes is your eternal Being.

181. Therefore stop identifying with the ephemeral body, with your family, your origin, your name, your education and your status. Also stop pretending you are the doer and the decision maker. Recognize your role as the essence of Being.

Jesus: If anyone comes to me and does not hate father and mother, wife and children, brothers and sisters – yes, even their own life – such a person cannot be my disciple.

Luke 14:26

Those are confusing words we read in the Gospel according to St. Luke. How should we behave toward our family, ourselves, our life? All four gospels prefer to use the language of allegories or images. Of course, the words above from St. Luke do not mean "hate" in the ordinary sense. We must not hate anyone to be liberated. To become a disciple of Jesus, we should end identifying with "mine" (my family, my success, my deeds, my specialty, my being better than others). Shankara uses other words, but the sentiment is the same.

True love knows no "mine", but only the oneness with all Being. To love means to recognize oneself in all things.

To be a "disciple of Jesus" or "to achieve the Atman" does not mean to love something, but to be love.

Jesus: But I say to you, love your enemies, bless those who curse you, do good to those who hate you, and pray for those who insult you and persecute you.
Matthew 5:44

Yoga and Samadhi

> *182. The concepts of "you", "I" or "this" are created by mistaken thoughts. In Samadhi, all these dualist distinctions are dissolved, and the only truth appears.*

Samadhi means the highest level of inner immersion. Patanjali, an Indian teacher of wisdom, said to have lived between the 2nd and 4th centuries A.D., is regarded as the author of the legendary "Yoga Sutras". They form the foundation for later yoga teachings, and they summarize the yoga knowledge of the time. In these Sutras, Samadhi is named as the last and highest goal of the yoga way which consists of eight levels.

> *183. Those who strive for liberation will rest carefully, patiently within themselves. In meditation, they are aware of oneness with all Being. Free of actions and movements of the mind, they enjoy the bliss of Brahman.*
>
> *184. Only those who reach Samadhi are disconnected from what ties them to the world. They are free from all karma. For them, the outer world, sensory perception, the mind and the ego flow into the Atman.*

The inner "I", also called "Self", becomes visible when all attributes of the external "I" fall aside. For that, we have to enter a thought-free space. This is extremely difficult for ordinary people, for whom it is the familiar normal condition of their consciousness to be thinking constantly.

We are obsessed with thinking. Since we identify with our sensory perception, our thoughts and feelings, we consider "non-thinking" a form of "non-existing". The ego will not and cannot accomplish that state. The ego, which is built upon concepts of thought, strongly objects to this. Without thoughts it loses the ground under its feet and plunges into an abyss – a terrible prospect for the ego.

As threatening and at the same time unimaginable as nonthinking may be for the ego, as free does the real "I am" feel when it practices non-thinking in meditation. Just being – not being this or that – is a redeeming, exhilarating experience.

185. The fabric of the supreme Self is very delicately woven and cannot be reached by materially oriented thoughts. That is why the mind first has to be placed in a subtle, highly responsive state through meditation.

186. Just as gold sheds its impurities in the heat of fire, the mind – through meditation – loses the cloudiness caused by Sattva, Rajas and Tamas.

187. Through constant exercise, we reach the highest level of meditation in which the mind connects with Brahman, the one without a second.

Basically, meditation is an easy route. What meditation means can be summarized with a few words: being present, attentive, free of thoughts, immersion in the Being.

188. In Samadhi, all desires are dissolved. That is when your inner nature can easily unfold inwardly and outwardly.

189. Contemplative thoughts are a hundred times more valuable than to just hear or read about Brahman. Meditation is a thousand times better than mere reflection. But Samadhi is unmatched in its effect.

In the first step, meditation means to observe what is present right now, and not to let the thoughts drift away into the past or the future. You observe everything your senses "now" perceive without attaching thoughts to it. You observe your breathing, you feel your body, you observe upcoming thoughts and feelings without letting them linger.

This kind of meditation can also be practiced during our ordinary daily routine, best while resting or during activities not demanding too much attention.

When we wish to focus entirely on meditation, we can proceed as follows: We find a quiet place. We go into the kind of sitting position in which we can remain awake for some time. We are as alert as possible. Best without thinking, we observe what is happening around us and inside us "right now". We pay attention to the thoughts and feelings as they come and go, without letting them carry us away. We are totally one with the present Being.

In the next step, we become aware of the observer. We recognize who is behind all the perception. We "see" the invisible observer who is always present within us. We connect with what is the essence of our Self: pure consciousness.

Only the observer can observe himself. The observer without contents is nothing but Atman. He is pure Being. The purpose of meditation is a state without thinking in which we experience oneness with Brahman.

Regular meditation will soon bring us enjoyable benefits. We calm down, become more balanced and composed. We are more and more able to remain in the here and now. We become more alert, our intuition improves ...

Some people think they have no time for meditation in addition to their worldly tasks. They do not realize that the time they spend for meditation will be paid back in quality – through more vitality and joy – as well as in quantity in the form of better decisions and better time management.

> *190. With Samadhi, the reality of Brahman becomes a permanent certainty.*
>
> *191. The first steps to yoga consist of mindful speech, a renunciation of property, absence of expectations, dispassion, and a reclusive life style.*
>
> *192. The purpose of a reclusive life style is to control the senses, which helps to observe the mind. Observing the mind leads to the abolishment of the ego. This all leads to the achievement of Brahman. That is why it is important always to observe the mind.*

Through repeated careful observation of our own thinking, it becomes brighter within us. A window opens on our wonderful Being, on what we really are, on our essence which is also the origin of the entire universe.

To "get hold" of our thinking, it is necessary to observe it from a distance again and again. We can only look at something properly when we are not part of it, chained to it and befuddled by it, but when we take a step back from it. That is how we gain distance to observe something at leisure. When we observe our thinking, the "thinker" liberates himself from thinking. We deliver ourselves from the stream of thoughts that is rushing along out of control.

Astronauts, who are privileged to look at our earth from space, rave about the beauty of this little ball in the big universe. Many objects appear wonderful and grand only when we look at them from a distance and in a more extensive way. When we do, the big and small everyday problems in which we are often helplessly entangled, will disappear.

193. Those who are firmly rooted in Brahman can easily end their external attachment on material objects and their internal attachment on the wishes of the ego.

194. Dispassion and distinction act like the two wings of a bird. You need both to reach the highest level of liberation.

195. Samadhi can be achieved only through a complete lack of desire. Only Samadhi caused lasting illumination and bliss.

Some people want to meditate to become illuminated and saintly "for" their ego. They want to add another special attribute to their external identity. Yet they overlook that this very intention prevents the fulfilment of their wish. Meditation is about "giving up" the ego, not about strengthening it. You may meditate for years, but if you only do it to achieve something for your ego, you will not make much progress.

Brahman is as the sky

196. As the wave, the surf, the whirlpool are in essence only water, everything in essence consists only of divine consciousness, from the body to the "I".

197. The entire universe perceived by the mind is nothing but Brahman; there is nothing outside Brahman, just as jugs and vessels of all kind consist only of clay. The distinction between "you" and "I" is only due to deception.

198. Brahman is as the sky, pure, absolute, unlimited, unmoved and unchanged. He encompasses the entire universe with all things.

Krishna: I am the everlasting self which dwells in all creatures. I am the origin of all, the way and also the goal.

Bhagavad Gita 10:20

Jesus: I am the way and the truth and the life.

John 14:6

In his thoughts, man can exclude himself from the completeness and beauty of Being. He thus becomes a seeker. Consciously or subconsciously, all people yearn for beauty, love, freedom, peace and fulfilment. Yet the seeker is like the little fish in the ocean looking for the sea. A big fish once told him of the enormous expanse, splendour and abundance of the sea, mocking him for the limited, "little fish" kind of life he was leading. Unfortunately, in his search, the little fish found much salt water and other things, but not the ocean, and therefore he is still longingly swimming around here and there without ever finding the wonderful sea.

Those who look with eyes that do not see the grand abundance of being but discover mainly defects and dangers, will live in fear. Their fear turns into the ego. The ego lives on desire, greed, envy, criticism and worries. Egotism springs from ignorance which leads to lack of faith. The world of the ego is oppressively small and narrow. Fear makes us fight for our fortune. There is little room for love, for the fear not to get enough and not to be loved enough hides the view of the completeness and beauty of Being. The more we struggle and thrash about, the murkier becomes the "water", preventing us from enjoying the expanse and abundance of the "ocean".

199. The first steps of recognition are worthless unless they are followed by others. Knowledge of Brahman solves all problems. Peace and supreme joy are the final award.

200. When the knot of ignorance in the heart has been cut, all desire for egoistical action ends, Brahman is revealed as love and bliss.

The universe was born of love! We do not need an "object" of love to be love. Love needs no love in return.

Love does not intend to do good. It simply radiates what it is. That makes it completely free. It needs no one to receive or return love. It has no expectations and therefore cannot be disappointed. It is simply joy and beauty, which it radiates without a care.

The sun also shines on land without life. The tree always offers shade, even when there is no one to enjoy its crown of leaves. The rose lends it beauty, if fragrance to everyone.

Love has no intention to benefit anyone. It is not proud of its merits. Love simply gives, regardless of praise, gratitude or recognition. It gives for the joy of giving.

Love is without expectation. It wants to possess no one, to make no one dependent, to control no one. Love is in harmony with the Being as it is.

Love does not care whether it is good enough and deserving enough. It is neither afraid of not winning anyone nor of losing someone. In such a way, love is one with the great peace.

201. Those who are connected with Brahman are completely aware and awake. They are without worry and delivered of all fear.

202. The liberated do not care about the past and waste no thought on the future. They calmly consider the present.

203. They look at all events with composure, whether they are good or bad, profit or loss, merit or failure.

204. They confront pleasant and painful experiences with the same serenity.

205. As the rivers that flow into the sea do not move the sea, thus the liberated remains untouched by all that happens in the apparent world. They always feel one with Brahman.

206. When we do good deeds or commit severe transgressions in a dream, we will neither go to heaven nor to hell. They end when we wake up.

207. By achieving our own identity with Brahman, all deeds and their consequences from countless previous lives will be wiped out just as the deeds in a dream end when we wake up.

208. The Atman is as free as the sky. Those who achieve it will no longer be pursued by the deeds of their past.

Karma and its dissolution

209. The pupil:
The consequences of karma someone has caused be-
fore becoming conscious cannot be cancelled when his
ignorance is removed. Even an arrow once shot upon an
object cannot be stopped in its flight.

210. An arrow presumably shot at a tiger cannot stop
when it realizes on its flight that its target is a cow.

211. The master speaks:
Indeed, even for a wise man, the consequences from the
past are so strong that he must bear them. Yet the fire of
recognition destroys all karma if the consequences have
not yet appeared.

212. Those who are always aware of their identity
with Brahman shall remain untouched on the inside
by the consequences from the past. To them, old karma
is meaningless, just as someone waking up from sleep
does not have to bother about the happenings in the
dream.

213. The body is formed by karma. But that is of no
concern to the Atman which is never touched by actions.

214. The causes of past actions are effective only as
long as we identify with the body. When we rise above
that, we are not affected by old karma.

As fire turns firewood into ashes, thus the fire of recognition burns the effect of all deeds.

Bhagavad Gita 4:37

215. *The best proof that a man has achieved Atman, the pure consciousness and bliss, is his own inner perception.*

216. *Only we ourselves can experience our attachment and liberation, inner peace and fear, health and hunger. Others can only draw conclusions about our inner state.*

217. *Teachers and scriptures can stimulate recognition. But only the pupil himself can overcome ignorance. He can be certain of help from the universal deity.*

218. *The liberated recognizes his invisible nature through his own fulfilment. Detached from worldly mirages he will stay in close connection with the Atman.*

The pupil experiences Brahman

219. The pupil, guided by the master, the scriptures and his own contemplations, begins to withdraw from the external world. With concentrated attention, he pauses in deepest peace and completely connects with the Atman/Brahman.

220. After he has remained for some time with Atman/ Brahman, he returns to normal consciousness and speaks:

221. My Mind and all its activities have entered the identity of Atman and Brahman. I cannot describe how boundless this joy is.

222. I felt like a hailstone falling into the expanse of the divine ocean while my mind dissolved in the delight of Brahman.

223. Where had the world gone? Who had removed it? What had it changed into? Had it stopped to exist? It is like a big miracle.

224. What can be accepted or refused in the ocean of Brahman which is filled with nectar?

225. I see nothing, I hear nothing, and I know nothing. I simply experience the absolute essence of joyful Being.

226. I thank you, my master, and I am grateful for the grace of Brahman.

227. I am blessed. I have reached the completeness of life. I am free from the chains of Samsara.

> *228. I am not the actor and not the one who harvests the fruits of his actions.*
>
> *229. I am free. I am at peace. I am without bounds, I am neither this nor that. I am the one without a second. I am incomparable, indestructible reality.*
>
> *230. Within me, the ocean of endless joy, the waves of the world are created and dissolved through the game of Maya.*
>
> *231. "Matter" and "time" are man's erroneous imagination. They divide the indivisible and fail to recognize timeless Being.*

Time is an illusion. It occurs in the state of separation from Brahman. The past is only an intellectual conception. No one has ever "experienced" the past. We can "experience" only the presence because there is only the timeless "Now". In the now, I can remember past "now moments". But the power of the presence is already absent from that memory. They are only "old" lifeless stories. Only the present moment is of any importance. Only in the now can we connect with our Self.

What has been said about the past also applies to the future. It, too, is an intellectual construction. We like to dwell in a fictitious future while turning away from the only reality, the Being in the presence. That is how we miss life. We do not live the blissful, always present dimension of Being.

> *"Time is what keep the light from reaching us. There is no greater obstacle on the path to God than time."*
> *Meister Eckehart*

We dream of the future because we expect it to deliver the fulfilment we cannot experience now. That is why in thought, we pursue the illusion of the future. We hope to achieve satisfaction in the future by chasing after it and by acting busily. But that dream never comes true because we can only be happy in the "Now". Connect today with your inner happiness!

Hopes, expectations, wishes, fears and worries lead to superfluous thinking of the future. Of course it makes sense to plan the day and to "make provisions". But usually this gets out of control and turns into "worrying". It is also prudent to learn from the past and to avoid repeating mistakes. But how often are we unnecessarily burdened by what was and by what we can no longer change? And many people like to worry about future events which as a rule will not turn out as anticipated.

232. Whatever the ignorant believe, even a large volume of water seen in a mirage cannot irrigate the desert.

233. I am as clear as the sky. I am as the sun and not like the things it illuminates; I remain as unmoved as a mountain and as boundlessly wide as the ocean.

Krishna: Space, time, heat and frost, joy and suffering are all formed through contact with the objects of the world. They come and go. They are without permanence. Face them with composure.
Bhagavad Gita 2:14

234. I have as little identity with the body as the sky has with the identity of clouds. How could such states as sleep, dreams or awakening touch me?

235. Experiences, deeds and characteristics of the ego come and go. They produce all kinds of fruits that are also ephemeral. In the meantime, I remain as untouched as a holy mountain.

In the world of forms, we cannot do without actions. As we read in the Bhagavad Gita (3:5): *"Thanks to the appearance of the world, we are all constantly forced to do something!"*

Even Krishna, the supreme God, says of himself: *"Even I, who is lacking nothing and who has to achieve nothing, am incessantly active."* (The Gita 3:22).

The visible as well as the invisible universe is always in motion. Everything lives, unfolds and develops.

On our spiritual way, we should by no means neglect our daily tasks. However, we will perform them with much more joy and effectiveness if we are connected with our inner dimension.

The wise man remains inwardly unmoved in acting and reposing.

236. How could deserving and negative results exist for me when I am not identical either with my body or my mind? I am unchangeable and without form, always untouched.

237. Heat and cold, good and bad might touch the shadow of my body, but never myself.

238. The characteristics of things and events do not touch the spectator who only observes them, just as the lamp is not touched by the objects it illuminates in a room.

239. Just as the sun is different than the things it illuminates, and fire is not identical with what it burns, I am the unchangeable Self.

240. Neither do I act myself nor do I let others act.

241. I am Brahman, the one without a second, the primal source of all Being. I make all things appear, and I illuminate them. Yet I am not touched by their diversity.

There is only "one" all-encompassing Being which also includes the external universe. The apparent universe is unimaginably vast, and even our most modern telescopes are unable to demonstrate its size. At the same time, its fundamental structures are infinitely small, much tinier than atoms. There are no researchable limits in either direction. These unimaginable sizes also reflect how endless our spiritual dimensions are. Only our thinking causes limits.

In spite of its endless expansion, the universe is only one. There are no two or more external worlds existing parallel to each other. Likewise, there is only one all-encompassing Being in the spiritual sense. That is also the origin of the belief in one all-encompassing God. Even the many gods we know from Hinduism and from the ancient Greeks form one "family" in "one" universe. And they are all united in Brahman.

242. I am Brahman who exceeds the endless forms of Maya. I am the essence of all.

243. Master, you have awakened me from sleep and saved me. I was caught in the jungle of birth and death. Day after day I was pursued by numerous problems and attacked by the tiger of egotism.

The supreme wisdom

I asked the wise old man:
Tell me the secrets of the world!
Softly he whispered, Hush! in my ear:
The silence will tell you, not words you can hear.
                                    Jalal Al-din Rumi

244. The master speaks:
All the world is only an expression of Brahman. Perceive
it with bright eyes and a clear mind!

245. What wise man would renounce the supreme bliss
for ephemeral things? When the magic moon is shining,
who would prefer to look at a painting of the moon?

246. Ephemeral, unreal things can neither provide
satisfaction nor end suffering. Therefore, remain in the
blissful state of identity with Brahman.

247. In all life situations, always remain connected
with your Self and enjoy the happiness that springs
from Brahman.

248. Dualist concepts of the world are like castles in the
air. Therefore, always remain aware of oneness with At-
man. That is how you overcome all fear, and how you
achieve love and supreme peace.

The opposite of inner peace is fear. It is the scourge of mankind.
It springs from ignorance about the completeness of being. In
the pure presence, in pure consciousness there is no fear. Fear
is the opposite of love. As it says in the First Epistle of John,

in the New Testament (1 John 4:18): *"There is no fear in love. But perfect love drives out fear."*

To those who do not perceive themselves as being one with the world, the world seems threatening. Fear is caused by a one-sided "I"-perspective. Those who repose in Atman do not know fear. The connection with Brahman and Atman is the true cure for all fear.

We can confront a real danger, which we very seldom face, more or less successfully. Usually we mistake situations, tasks and challenges with dangers. The mind likes to imagine what terrible things could happen in the future. Fear of the future is the terrible thing, not what might happen in the future.

249. If you recognize Brahman, your mind will be liberated from restless doing.

250. Those who achieve their own nature will feel the bliss of Brahman within them in all situations, whether they are walking or standing, sitting or lying down. They will savour being without want.

251. They will no longer depend on conditions of locality, time, religious denomination, moral rules or certain objects of meditation. The will only follow the voice of their Self.

The lovers of God have no religion but God alone.
Jalal Al-din Rumi

252. The Atman, which represents eternal truth, appears as soon as there is real insight. You need no special place or a certain time or certain rituals of purification.

253. The Atman can only reveal itself just as the sun is not illuminated by another light. The sacred scriptures also owe their wisdom to the Atman alone.

Unfounded love

254. Material things neither worry nor inspire the At-man. It neither depends on them nor is it inclined against them. It is love without desire.

255. Children are devoted to playing with their toys, forgetting hunger and worries. That is how the awakened enjoys Being, no longer burdened by ideas like "I" and "mine".

Love without a reason knows neither "I" nor "mine".

Real love has no reason and no "because" ...When I love "because I like someone or something"; "because "someone is nice to me, understands me, praises me", this is only a reaction to something pleasant. There is nothing wrong with being happy about praise, and it is good and makes sense to pay others respect. But being dependent on praise destroys love. "Love without reason" needs no cause, no object.

Love can only unfold where the fearful ego is silent. "Devotion" provides room for love. In devotion we find ourselves.

There are different forms of devotion: Devotion to a task, to the beauty of nature, to people. We can devote ourselves to a conversation or only to the present moment.

Love means losing one's ego. It means abandoning expectations, wishes, desire and dependence, fears and hopes. That is why so many people avoid entering a close relationship.

There are two ways of "love". In one kind the "I" wants to have something for itself. It wants to be praised, loved and desired. It demands that the other party satisfies its expectations. That is why this kind of love is afraid and jealous. As soon as the other is not behaving the way the "I" wants, disappointment spreads, and the heart suffers a cut, a pain, that becomes a burden for the continued relationship.

In a true relationship, two "non-I" persons meet. These two "I's" have no expectations and no disappointments. The ego love yearns for this unconditional, comprehensive love, but at the same time it does not want to let go its own wishes and worries. Letting go means for it losing its ego feeling. But the ego prefers to cling to hopes and suffers disappointments rather than abandoning itself to nothing and everything.

If only the ego knew it will receive everything if it can let go of everything.

The knower of Atman

256. The knower of Atman does not depend on external things. He does not attract attention with special clothing. He reposes in his body without identification. He enjoys material objects as they come and go.

257. He wanders about in the world in a variety of clothing. He sometimes appears as a crazy man, other times as a sage. He will be honoured sometimes, ridiculed at other times. He is not concerned about anything.

258. He has no riches and yet he is satisfied. He sometimes seems helpless, and yet he is full of strength. He is always full of joy. He resembles no one, and yet he does not feel special.

259. He acts, but he is not active. He earns the fruits of his past labours and is yet untouched by them. He has a body, but does not identify with it. He seems to be alone and is yet connected with all.

260. The knower of Brahman is touched by neither pleasure nor suffering, neither good nor bad.

261. Ignorant people identify the liberated with his body. He himself regards this body as a snake regards its shed skin.

262. The fulfilled sees the movements of his body as a witness, free of mental fluctuations.

263. Dependence as well as liberation are illusions of Maya. They do not really exist.

None of our mistakes and errors are of importance because miscreations of the mind do not really exist – although we are suffering from them.

We can speak of dependence and liberation only at the dualist level. The illusion of dependence and liberation is created by Maya. These distinctions dissolve when we go beyond thinking and become immersed in the depth of present Being.

What is true is everlasting – nothing unreal exists.

> *If you could only free yourselves of thinking in concepts and visualizations, you would have achieved everything.*
>
> *Huang Po*

> *264. People speak of dependence when there is a veil of ignorance. To them, liberation means the end of ignorance. Yet Brahman is beyond such distinctions. In reality there is no veil, just Brahman.*
>
> *265. There is neither death nor birth, neither a soul struggling with difficulties nor an enlightened soul, nor a seeker for liberation nor a liberated. That is the supreme wisdom.*

Some fragments of thought by the translator

It has been a great pleasure and privilege to translate The Crown Jewel of Distinction, newly mounted by Bernd Helge Fritsch, from German into English. It has also been an emotional experience, a source of much wisdom and insight.

While it has been enjoyable and thought-provoking to translate the "mounting", i.e. the explanatory and thought-provoking framework provided by this book's author, translating Adi Shankara's texts – not from 9th century Sanskrit, but from 21st century German – into modern English has been the greatest challenge and the most satisfying part of the work.

I tried to render the text as accurately as possible to let English readers have the maximum benefit not only of Shankara's wisdom but also of Fritsch's helpful additional texts. I also hope to have achieved what I consider the most important aspect of literary translation, the preservation of what French philosopher and linguist Roland Barthes called "le bruissement de la langue".(German: das Rauschen der Sprache, which some have called"the rustle of language" in English, although I prefer to call it"the murmur of language").

I was fortunate to benefit from many discussions with the book's author about concepts and nuances and precise intentions of expression. Yet most astonishing was the distinct feeling – especially when burning the midnight oil – to have the Indian master himself tap me on the shoulder and inspire me to use this and not that phrase, this and not that word. Of course I realized that it wasn't Adi who tapped me, but I am now almost certain it was his Atman. Together, I hope we have provided the reader with just the right murmur of language.

Index

Recommended books

"The Essence
of the Bhagavad Gita"

Bernd Helge Fritsch

This book results from the author's decades of in-depth studies of Eastern spirituality.

The Bhagavad Gita combines the most beautiful pearls of Ancient Indian wisdom into a wonderful entity. The "Song of the Sublime" thoroughly explains all the important subjects of the earthly and the divine world.

The Gita provides us with one of the most valuable and beautiful revelations mankind has ever received. Its verses open a gate to spiritual self-recognition and to a discovery of the divine.

This edition of the Gita offers today's readers a most practical access to its essence thanks to a careful selection of all important text passages and the use of clear, easily understandable language. Comments added to the translation will facilitate a deep understanding of this ancient and yet timeless eastern teaching.

Buchempfehlung

"Der große Prinz
und das Glück"

Bernd Helge Fritsch

Rund 80 Jahre nachdem Antoine de Saint-Exupéry, Schriftsteller und Flugpilot, dem "Kleinen Prinz" in einer afrikanischen Wüste begegnen durfte, erscheint wieder ein "Prinz" von einem andern Stern auf unserer Erde. Es ist der "Große Prinz", der hier auf unserem Planeten das Leben und das Glück der Menschen studiert.

In diesem Buch wurden seine Erfahrungen und Erkenntnisse über das "Glücklich-Sein" niedergeschrieben.

Ein Buch, das uns das "WunderLeben" mit neuen
Augen betrachten lässt.

Ein Buch, das uns dem Geheimnis eines *"tiefen und
anhaltenden Glücklich-Seins"* näher bringt.

Buchempfehlung

Vom Umgang mit der Zeit
99 spirituelle Anregungen

Bernd H. Fritsch

In diesem Hand-Buch findest du 99 Aphorismen für ein "Leben in der Zeit und in der Zeitlosigkeit".

Alle wesentlichen Lebensbereiche des Menschen, wie beispielsweise: Liebe, Freundschaft, Gesundheit, Freude, Umgang mit Konflikten, Beendigung von Schuldgefühlen, Fehler machen dürfen... werden in diesen Aphorismen in prägnanter und gut verständlicher Weise angesprochen. Ein idealer Begleiter um sich zu besinnen, um auf deinem Weg das Wesentliche vom Unwesentlichen zu unterscheiden.

Du findest in diesem Brevier leicht lesbare Anregungen zu einem Leben in Frieden und Vollkommenheit, frei von Zeitdruck, Stress, Ängsten und Sorgen.

Aufgezeigt wird, wie durch die Erkenntnis des Sinns unseres Daseins und durch die richtige Einstellung zu unseren Aufgaben, jeder Augenblick unseres Erdenleben etwas Besonderes sein kann.

Der Autor hat in diesem kleinen Büchlein all seine, im Laufe von rund sieben Jahrzehnten gewonnenen Erkenntnisse, zusammengefasst. Für den, der bereit ist sich auf die Weisheiten in dieser Schrift einzulassen, werden sich neue Dimensionen eröffnen.

Buchempfehlung

WU-WEI
erfolgreich Nichts tun

Bernd Helge Fritsch

Dieses Buch beinhaltet eine Auswahl von Essay-Briefen, wie sie von Bernd Helge Fritsch seit etlichen Jahren in Mail-Form an Freunde und Interessierte versendet werden. Diese Briefe behandeln die wichtigsten Lebensfragen. Zu diesen zähle ich:

- Was ist der Sinn unseres Erdendaseins?
- Wer bin ich?
- Wie lebt man erfüllende Beziehungen?
- Vom Umgang mit Depressionen
- Wie kann ich glücklich sein, unabhängig von äußeren Ereignissen?
- Was geschieht mit mir nach meinem körperlichen Tod?

Diese Essay-Briefe sollen keine "Glaubensinhalte" vermitteln. Der Autor möchte kein "gläubiger Mensch" sein und gehört deshalb auch keiner Religionsgemeinschaft an. Wohl aber ist nach seiner Ansicht "Religion" (die bewusste Verbindung mit dem Höchsten) unsere wichtigste Mission auf dieser Erde.

Please write to us!

Please write to us!

Please write to us if you......

- ....want to ask the author, Bernd Helge Fritsch, any questions;

- ....are prepared to give us suggestions and feed-back;

- ....want to have information about lectures and seminars by Bernd Helge Fritsch;

- ....want to receive our free monthly "Essay Letter" by email.

We welcome every letter or message and will be happy to reply.

Email: office@berndhelgefritsch.com

Visit our homepage:
www.berndhelgefritsch.com